D0440821

HBR Guide to
Emotional Intelligence

Harvard Business Review Guides

Arm yourself with the advice you need to succeed on the job, from the most trusted brand in business. Packed with how-to essentials from leading experts, the HBR Guides provide smart answers to your most pressing work challenges.

The titles include:

HBR Guide to Being More Productive

HBR Guide to Better Business Writing

HBR Guide to Building Your Business Case

HBR Guide to Buying a Small Business

HBR Guide to Coaching Employees

HBR Guide to Data Analytics Basics for Managers

HBR Guide to Delivering Effective Feedback

HBR Guide to Emotional Intelligence

HBR Guide to Finance Basics for Managers

HBR Guide to Getting the Right Work Done

HBR Guide to Leading Teams

HBR Guide to Making Every Meeting Matter

HBR Guide to Managing Stress at Work

HBR Guide to Managing Up and Across

HBR Guide to Negotiating

HBR Guide to Office Politics

HBR Guide to Performance Management

HBR Guide to Persuasive Presentations

HBR Guide to Project Management

HBR Guide to
Emotional Intelligence

HARVARD BUSINESS REVIEW PRESS

Boston, Massachusetts

Copyright 2017 Harvard Business School Publishing Corporation

Library of Congress cataloging-in-publication data is forthcoming.

ISBN: 9781633692725
eISBN: 9781633692732

The paper used in this publication meets the requirements of the American National Standard for Permanence of Paper for Publications and Documents in Libraries and Archives Z39.48-1992.

What You'll Learn

It's been two decades since Daniel Goleman's research showed that emotional intelligence is twice as important as other skills in determining outstanding leadership. By managing your emotions and relating well to others, he explained, you can achieve higher levels of influence as well as personal well-being.

This kind of emotional intelligence is not just an innate trait: It can be learned. Becoming more finely attuned to your own emotions allows you to determine how to use those feelings more productively to make stronger decisions, overcome negative thoughts, control yourself in volatile situations, or understand others when they act in a way that surprises or angers you. Getting feedback from trusted colleagues and friends can keep you honest and aware of your areas of weakness, especially in the social sphere. And whether you're writing a difficult email, looking to keep your cool in a bitter negotiation, or managing an upset direct report, an array of frameworks and tactics can help you approach the situation in a way that takes the human element into account.

This guide will help you navigate these approaches. You'll get better at:

- Identifying and managing your own emotions

- Persuading and influencing others

- Dealing with difficult colleagues

- Responding to stress productively

- Defusing tense conversations

- Using your feelings as data to help you make smarter decisions

- Avoiding emotional pitfalls in a negotiation

- Reacting to tough situations with resilience

- Helping others on your team develop their emotional intelligence

- Developing a strong emotional culture

Contents

Table of Contents

SECTION FIVE

Dealing with Difficult People

What Is Emotional Intelligence?

CHAPTER 1

Leading by Feel

Like it or not, leaders need to manage the mood of their organizations. The most gifted leaders accomplish that by using a mysterious blend of psychological abilities known as *emotional intelligence*. They're self-aware and empathetic. They can read and regulate their own emotions while intuitively grasping how others feel and gauging their organization's emotional state.

But where does emotional intelligence come from? And how do leaders learn to use it? The management literature (and even common sense) suggests that both nature and nurture feed emotional intelligence. Part genetic predisposition, part life experience, and part old-fashioned training, emotional intelligence emerges in varying degrees from one leader to the next,

Excerpted from *Harvard Business Review*, January 2004 (product #R0401B)

and managers apply it with varying skill. Wisely and compassionately deployed, emotional intelligence spurs leaders, their people, and their organizations to superior performance; naively or maliciously applied, it can paralyze leaders or allow them to manipulate followers for personal gain.

We invited 18 leaders and scholars (including business executives, leadership researchers, psychologists, a neurologist, a cult expert, and a symphony conductor) to explore the nature and management of emotional intelligence—its sources, uses, and abuses. Their responses differed dramatically, but there were some common themes: the importance of consciously and conscientiously honing one's skills, the double-edged nature of self-awareness, and the danger of letting any one emotional intelligence skill dominate. Here are some of their perspectives.

Be Realistic

John D. Mayer *is a professor of psychology at the University of New Hampshire. He and Yale psychology professor Peter Salovey are credited with first defining the concept of emotional intelligence in the early 1990s.*

This is a time of growing realism about emotional intelligence—especially concerning what it is and what it isn't. The books and articles that have helped popularize the concept have defined it as a loose collection of personality traits, such as self-awareness, optimism, and tolerance. These popular definitions have been accompanied by exaggerated claims about the importance of emotional intelligence. But diverse personality traits, however admirable, don't necessarily add up to a single definition of emotional intelligence. In fact, such traits are difficult to collectively evaluate in a way that reveals their relationship to success in business and in life.

Even when they're viewed in isolation, the characteristics commonly associated with emotional intelligence and success may be more complicated than they seem. For example, the scientific jury is out on how important self-awareness is to successful leadership. In fact, too much self-awareness can reduce self-esteem, which is often a crucial component of great leadership.

From a scientific standpoint, emotional intelligence is the ability to accurately perceive your own and others' emotions; to understand the signals that emotions send about relationships; and to manage your own and others' emotions. It doesn't necessarily include the qualities (like optimism, initiative, and self-confidence) that some popular definitions ascribe to it.

Researchers have used performance tests to measure people's accuracy at identifying and understanding emotions; for example, asking them to identify the emotions conveyed by a face or which among several situations is most likely to bring about happiness. People who get high scores on these tests are indeed different from others. In the business world, they appear better able to deal with customers' complaints or to mediate disputes, and they may excel at making strong and positive personal connections with subordinates and customers over the long term. Of course, emotional intelligence isn't the only way to attain success as a leader: A brilliant strategist who can maximize profits may be able to hire and keep talented employees even if he or she doesn't have strong personal connections with them.

Is there value in scales that, based on popular conceptions, measure qualities like optimism and self-confidence but label them "emotional intelligence"? Certainly, these personality traits are important in business, so measuring and (sometimes) enhancing them can be useful. But recent research makes it clear that these characteristics are distinct from emotional intelligence as it is scientifically defined. A person high in emotional intelligence may be realistic rather than optimistic and insecure rather than confident. Conversely, a person may be highly self-confident and optimistic but lack emotional intelligence. The danger lies in assuming that because a person is optimistic or confident, they are also emotionally intelligent, when, in fact, the presence of those traits will tell you nothing of the sort.

Never Stop Learning

Daniel Goleman *is the cochair of the Consortium for Research on Emotional Intelligence in Organizations based at Rutgers University's Graduate School of Applied and Professional Psychology in Piscataway, New Jersey.*

You can be a successful leader without much emotional intelligence if you're extremely lucky and you've got everything else going for you: booming markets, bumbling competitors, and clueless higher-ups. If you're incredibly smart, you can cover for an absence of emotional intelligence until things get tough for the business.

But at that point, you won't have built up the social capital needed to pull the best out of people under tremendous pressure. The art of sustained leadership is getting others to produce superior work, and high IQ alone is insufficient to that task.

The good news is that emotional intelligence can be learned and improved at any age. In fact, data shows that, on average, people's emotional intelligence tends to increase as they age. But the specific leadership competencies that are based on emotional intelligence don't necessarily come through life experience. For example, one of the most common complaints I hear about leaders, particularly newly promoted ones, is that they lack empathy. The problem is that they were promoted because they were outstanding individual performers—and being a solo achiever doesn't teach you the skills necessary to understand other people's concerns.

Leaders who are motivated to improve their emotional intelligence can do so if they're given the right *information, guidance,* and *support.* The information they need is a candid assessment of their strengths and limitations from people who know them well and whose opinions they trust. The guidance they need is a specific developmental plan that uses naturally occurring workplace encounters as the laboratory for learning. The support they need is someone to talk to as they practice how to handle different situations, what to do when they've blown it, and how to learn from those setbacks. If leaders cultivate these resources and practice continually, they can develop specific emotional intelligence skills— skills that will last for years.

5 COMPONENTS OF EMOTIONAL INTELLIGENCE

In 1998, in what has become one of HBR's most enduring articles, "What Makes a Leader?" Daniel Goleman
introduced a framework of five components of emotional intelligence that allow individuals to recognize,
connect with, and learn from their own and other people's mental states, as well as their hallmarks. While
there are many frameworks offering varying sets of
EI competencies (and other models that conceive of
emotional intelligence not as a set of competencies
but rather as the ability to abstract and problem solve
in the emotional domain), Goleman's approach, out-
lined in exhibit 1, can be a helpful way to start building
an understanding of emotional intelligence:

EXHIBIT 1

EI Component	Definition	Hallmarks	Example
Self-awareness	Knowing one's emotions, strengths, weaknesses, drives, values, and goals—and their impacts on others	• Self-confidence • Realistic self-assessment • Self-deprecating sense of humor • Thirst for constructive criticism	A manager knows tight deadlines bring out the worst in him. So he plans his time to get work done well in advance.
Self-regulation	Controlling or redirecting disruptive emotions and impulses	• Trustworthiness • Integrity • Comfort with ambiguity and change	When a team botches a presentation, its leader resists the urge to scream. Instead, she considers possible reasons for the failure, explains the consequences to her team, and explores solutions with them.

EI Component	Definition	Hallmarks	Example
Motivation	Being driven to achieve for the sake of achievement	• A passion for the work itself and for new challenges • Unflagging energy to improve • Optimism in the face of failure	A portfolio manager at an investment company sees his fund tumble for three consecutive quarters. Major clients defect. Instead of blaming external circumstances, she decides to learn from the experience—and engineers a turnaround.
Empathy	Considering others' feelings, especially when making decisions	• Expertise in attracting and retaining talent • Ability to develop others • Sensitivity to cross-cultural differences	An American consultant and her team pitch a project to a potential client in Japan. Her team interprets the client's silence as disapproval and prepares to leave. The consultant reads the client's body language and senses interest. She continues the meeting, and her team gets the job.
Social skill	Managing relationships to move in desired directions	• Effectiveness in leading change • Persuasiveness • Extensive networking • Expertise in building and leading teams	A manager wants his company to adopt a better internet strategy. He finds kindred spirits and assembles a de facto team to create a prototype website. He persuades allies in other divisions to fund the company's participation in a relevant convention. His company forms an internet division—and puts him in charge of it.

Adapted from "What Makes a Leader" by Daniel Goleman, originally published in *Harvard Business Review*, June 2006.

Get Motivated

Richard Boyatzis *is a professor and the chair of the department of organizational behavior at Case Western Reserve University's Weatherhead School of Management in Cleveland.*

People can develop their emotional intelligence if they really want to. But many managers jump to the conclusion that their complement of emotional intelligence is predetermined. They think, "I could never be good at this, so why bother?" The central issue isn't a lack of *ability* to change; it's the lack of *motivation* to change.

Leadership development is not all that different from other areas in which people are trying to change their behaviors. Just look at the treatments for alcoholism, drug addiction, and weight loss: They all require the desire to change. More subtly, they all require a positive, rather than a negative, motivation. You have to *want* to change. If you think you'll lose your job because you're not adequately tuned in to your employees, you might become determinedly empathetic or compassionate for a time. But change driven by fear or avoidance probably isn't going to last. Change driven by hopes and aspirations, change that's pursued because it's desired, will be more enduring.

There's no such thing as having too much emotional intelligence. But there is a danger in being preoccupied with, or overusing, one aspect of it. For example, if you overemphasize the emotional intelligence competencies of initiative or achievement, you'll always be changing things at your company. Nobody would know what you were going to do next, which would be quite destabilizing for the organization. If you overuse empathy, you might never fire anybody. If you overuse teamwork, you might never build diversity or listen to a lone voice. Balance is essential.

Train the Gifted

Elkhonon Goldberg *is a clinical professor of neurology at New York University School of Medicine and the director of the Institute of Neuropsychology and Cognitive Performance in New York.*

In the past, neuropsychologists were mostly concerned with cognitive impairment. Today, they are increasingly interested in the biological underpinnings of cognitive differences in people without impairments—including differences in people's emotional intelligence.

Emotional intelligence can be learned, to a degree. It's like mathematical or musical ability. Can you become a musician if you lack natural aptitude? Yes, you can, if you take lessons and practice enough. But will you ever be a Mozart? Probably not. In the same way, emotional intelligence develops through a combination of biological endowment and training. And people who don't have that endowment probably won't become deeply emotionally intelligent just through training. Trying to drum emotional intelligence into someone with no aptitude for it is an exercise in futility. I believe the best way to get emotionally intelligent leaders is to select for people who already show the basic qualities you want. Think about it: That's how athletic coaches operate. They don't just work with anyone who wants to play a sport; they train the naturally gifted. Business managers should do the same.

How do you identify the naturally gifted? I'd say you have to look for those with a genuine, instinctive interest in other people's experiences and mental worlds. It's an absolute prerequisite for developing emotional intelligence. If a manager lacks this interest, maybe your training resources are better directed elsewhere.

Seek Frank Feedback

Andrea Jung *is the chair and CEO of Avon Products, which is based in New York.*

Emotional intelligence is in our DNA here at Avon because relationships are critical at every stage of our business. It starts with the relationships our 4.5 million independent sales reps have with their customers and goes right up through senior management to my office. So the emphasis on emotional intelligence is much greater here than it was at other companies in which I've worked. We incorporate emotional intelligence education into our development training for senior managers, and we factor in emotional intelligence competencies when we evaluate employees' performance.

Of all a leader's competencies, emotional and otherwise, self-awareness is the most important. Without it, you can't identify the impact you have on others. Self-awareness is very important for me as CEO. At my level, few people are willing to tell me the things that are hardest to hear. We have a CEO advisory counsel—ten people chosen each year from Avon offices throughout the world—and they tell me the good, the bad, and the ugly about the company. Anything can be said. It helps keep me connected to what people really think and how my actions affect them. I also rely on my children for honest appraisals. You can get a huge dose of reality by seeing yourself through your children's eyes, noticing the ways they react to and reflect what you say and do. My kids are part of my 360-degree feedback. They're the most honest of all.

I grew up in a very traditional Chinese family. My parents were concerned that the way I'd been raised—submissive, caring, and averse to conflict—would hinder my ability to succeed in the *Fortune* 500 environment. They were afraid I couldn't make the tough decisions. But I've learned how to be empathetic and still make hard decisions that are right for the company. These are not incompatible abilities. When Avon has had to close plants, for example, I've tried to act with compassion for the people involved. And I've gotten letters from some of the associates who were affected, expressing sadness but also saying thanks for the fair treatment. Leaders' use of emotional intelligence when making tough decisions is important to their success—and to the success of their organizations.

Engage Your Demons

David Gergen *directs the Center for Public Leadership at Harvard University's John F. Kennedy School of Government in Cambridge, Massachusetts. He served as an adviser to presidents Nixon, Ford, Reagan, and Clinton.*

American history suggests not only that emotional intelligence is an indispensable ingredient of political leadership but also that it can be enhanced through sustained effort. George Washington had to work hard to control his fiery temper before he became a role model for the republic, and Abraham Lincoln had to overcome deep melancholia to display the brave and warm countenance that made him a magnet for others. Franklin Delano Roosevelt provides an even more graphic example: In his early adult years, FDR seemed carefree and condescending. Then, at 39, he was stricken with polio. By most accounts, he transformed himself over the next seven years of struggle into a leader of empathy, patience, and keen self-awareness.

Richard Nixon thought he might transform himself through his own years in the wilderness, and he did make progress. But he could never fully control his demons, and they eventually brought him down. Bill Clinton, too, struggled for self-mastery and made progress, but he could not fully close the cracks in his character, and he paid a stiff price. Not all people succeed, then, in achieving self-awareness and self-control. What we have been told since the time of the Greeks is that every leader must try to control his own passions before he can hope to command the passions of others.

Best-selling author Rabbi Harold Kushner argues persuasively that the elements of selfishness and aggression that are in most of us—and our struggles to overcome them—are exactly what make for better leadership. In *Living a Life That Matters*, Kushner writes of the personal torments of leaders from Jacob, who wrestled all night with an angel, to Martin Luther King Jr., who tried to cleanse himself of weakness even as he cleansed the nation's soul. "Good people do bad things," Kushner concludes, "If they weren't mightily tempted by their *yetzer ha'ra* [will to do evil], they might not be capable of the mightily good things they do."

Find Your Voice

William George *is the former chairman and CEO of Medtronic, a medical technology company in Minneapolis.*

Authentic leadership begins with self-awareness, or knowing yourself deeply. Self-awareness is not a trait you are born with but a capacity you develop throughout your lifetime. It's your understanding of your strengths and weaknesses, your purpose in life, your values and motivations, and how and why you respond to situations in a particular way. It requires a great deal of introspection and the ability to internalize feedback from others.

No one is born a leader; we have to consciously develop into the leader we want to become. It takes many years of hard work and the ability to learn from extreme difficulties and disappointments. But in their scramble to get ahead, many would-be leaders attempt to skip this crucial developmental stage. Some of these people do get to the top of companies through sheer determination and aggressiveness. However, when they finally reach the leader's chair, they can be very destructive because they haven't focused on the hard work of personal development.

To mask their inadequacies, these leaders tend to close themselves off, cultivating an image or persona rather than opening up to others. They often adopt the styles of other leaders they have observed.

Leaders who are driven to achieve by shortcomings in their character, for example, or a desire for self-aggrandizement, may take inordinate risks on behalf of the organization. They may even come to believe they are so important that they place their interests above those of the organization.

Self-awareness and other emotional intelligence skills come naturally to some, less so to others—but these skills can be learned. One of the techniques I have found most useful in gaining deeper self-awareness is meditation. In 1975, my wife dragged me, kicking and screaming, to a weekend course in Transcendental Meditation. I have meditated 20 minutes, twice a day, ever since. Meditation makes me calmer, more focused, and better able to discern what's really important. Leaders, by the very nature of their positions, are under extreme pressure to keep up with the many voices clamoring for their attention. Indeed, many leaders lose their way. It is only through a deep self-awareness that you can find your inner voice and listen to it.

Know the Score

Michael Tilson Thomas *is the music director of the San Francisco Symphony.*

A conductor's authority rests on two things: the orchestra's confidence in the conductor's insightful knowledge of the whole score; and the orchestra's faith in the conductor's good heart, which seeks to inspire everyone to make music that is excellent, generous, and sincere.

Old-school conductors liked to hold the lead in their hands at all times. I do not. Sometimes I lead. Other times I'll say, "Violas, I'm giving you the lead. Listen to one another; and find your way with this phrase." I'm not trying to drill people, military style, to play music exactly together. I'm trying to encourage them to play as one, which is a different thing. I'm guiding the performance, but I'm aware that they're executing it. It's their sinews, their heartstrings. I'm there to help them do it in a way that is convincing and natural for them but also a part of the larger design.

My approach is to be in tune with the people with whom I'm working. If I'm conducting an ensemble for the first time, I will relate what I want them to do to the great things they've already done. If I'm conducting my own orchestra, I can see in the musicians' bodies and faces how they're feeling that day, and it becomes very clear who may need encouragement and who may need cautioning.

The objectivity and perspective I have as the only person who is just listening is a powerful thing. I try to use this perspective to help the ensemble reach its goals.

Keep It Honest

Carol Bartz *is the chairman, president, and CEO of Autodesk, a design software and digital content company in San Rafael, California.*

A friend needed to take a six-month assignment in a different part of the country. She had an ancient, ill, balding but beloved dog that she could not take with her. Her choices boiled down to boarding the poor animal, at enormous expense, or putting it out of its obvious misery. Friends said, "Board the dog," though behind my friend's back, they ridiculed that option. She asked me what I thought, and I told her, kindly but clearly, that I thought she should have the dog put to sleep rather than spend her money keeping it in an environment where it would be miserable and perhaps die anyway. My friend was furious with me for saying this. She boarded the dog and went away on her assignment. When she returned, the dog was at death's door and had to be put to sleep. Not long after that, my friend came around to say thanks. "You were the only person who told me the truth," she said. She came to appreciate that I had cared enough to tell her what I thought was best, even if what I said hurt at the time.

That event validated a hunch that has stood me in good stead as I've led my company. Empathy and compassion have to be balanced with honesty. I have pulled people into my office and told them to deal with certain issues for the sake of themselves and their teams. If they are willing to learn, they will say, "Gee, no one ever told me." If they are unwilling, they're not right for this organization. And I must let them go for the sake of the greater good.

Go for the Gemba

Hirotaka Takeuchi *is the dean of Hitotsubashi University's Graduate School of International Corporate Strategy in Tokyo.*

Self-awareness, self-control, empathy, humility, and other such emotional intelligence traits are particularly important in Asia. They are part of our Confucian emphasis on *wah*, or social harmony. When books on emotional intelligence were first translated into Japanese, people said, "We already know that. We're actually trying to get beyond that." We've been so focused on wah that we've built up a supersensitive structure of social niceties, where everyone seeks consensus. In the Japanese hierarchy, everyone knows his or her place, so no one is ever humiliated. This social supersensitivity—itself a form of emotional intelligence—can lead people to shy away from conflict. But conflict is often the only way to get to the *gemba*—the front line, where the action really is, where the truth lies.

Thus, effective management often depends not on coolly and expertly resolving conflict—or simply avoiding it—but on embracing it at the gemba. Japan's most effective leaders do both. The best example is Nissan's Carlos Ghosn. He not only had the social skills to listen to people and win them over to his ideas, but he also dared to lift the lid on the corporate hierarchy and encourage people at all levels of the organization to offer suggestions to operational, organizational, and even interpersonal problems—even if that created conflict. People were no longer suppressed, so solutions to the company's problems bubbled up.

Balance the Load

Linda Stone *is the former vice president of corporate and industry initiatives at Microsoft in Redmond, Washington.*

Emotional intelligence is powerful—which is precisely why it can be dangerous. For example, empathy is an extraordinary relationship-building tool, but it must be used skillfully or it can do serious damage to the person doing the empathizing. In my case, overdoing empathy took a physical toll. In May 2000, Steve Ballmer charged me with rebuilding Microsoft's industry relationships, a position that I sometimes referred to as "chief listening officer." The job was part ombudsperson, part new initiatives developer, part pattern recognizer, and part rapid-response person. In the first few months of the job—when criticism of the company was at an all-time high—it became clear that this position was a lightning rod. I threw myself into listening and repairing wherever I could.

Within a few months, I was exhausted from the effort. I gained a significant amount of weight, which, tests finally revealed, was probably caused by a hormone imbalance partially brought on by stress and lack of sleep. In absorbing everyone's complaints, perhaps to the extreme, I had compromised my health. This was a wake-up call: I needed to reframe the job.

I focused on connecting the people who needed to work together to resolve problems rather than taking on each repair myself. I persuaded key people inside the company to listen and work directly with important people outside the company, even in cases where the internal folks were skeptical at first about the need for this direct connection. In a sense, I tempered my empathy and ratcheted up relationship building. Ultimately, with a wiser and more balanced use of empathy, I became more effective and less stressed in my role.

Question Authority

Ronald Heifetz *is a cofounder of the Center for Public Leadership at Harvard University's John F. Kennedy School of Government in Cambridge, Massachusetts, and a partner at Cambridge Leadership Associates, a consultancy in Cambridge.*

Emotional intelligence is necessary for leadership but not sufficient. Many people have some degree of emotional intelligence and can indeed empathize with and rouse followers; a few of them can even generate great charismatic authority. But I would argue that if they are using emotional intelligence solely to gain formal or informal authority, that's not leadership at all. They are using their emotional intelligence to grasp what people want, only to pander to those desires in order to gain authority and influence. Easy answers sell.

Leadership couples emotional intelligence with the courage to raise the tough questions, challenge people's assumptions about strategy and operations—and risk losing their goodwill. It demands a commitment to serving others; skill at diagnostic, strategic, and tactical reasoning; the guts to get beneath the surface of tough realities; and the heart to take heat and grief.

For example, David Duke did an extraordinary job of convincing Ku Klux Klan members to get out of their backyards and into hotel conference rooms. He brought his considerable emotional intelligence to bear, his capacity to empathize with his followers, to pluck their heartstrings in a powerful way that mobilized them. But he avoided asking his people the tough questions: Does our program actually solve our problem? How will creating a social structure of white supremacy give us the self-esteem we lack? How will it solve the problems of poverty, alcoholism, and family violence that corrode our sense of self-worth?

Like Duke, many people with high emotional intelligence and charismatic authority aren't interested in asking the deeper questions, because they get so much emotional gain from the adoring crowd. For them, that's the end in itself. They're satisfying their own hungers and vulnerabilities: their need to be liked; their need for power and control; or their need to be needed, to feel important, which renders them vulnerable to grandiosity. But that's not primal leadership. It's primal hunger for authority.

Maintaining one's primacy or position is not in and of itself leadership, however inspiring it may seem to be. Gaining primal authority is relatively easy.

CHAPTER 2

Do You Lead with Emotional Intelligence?

by Annie McKee

Great leaders move us—they inspire, motivate, and energize us. How? They do it through emotional intelligence. Dan Goleman woke us all up when he published his groundbreaking book on the topic (in 1995). Since then we've learned a lot about EI competencies, such as self-awareness and empathy, and about what people can do to develop them. To gain a deeper understanding of your own emotional intelligence, respond to the statements in this questionnaire as honestly as possible, checking one of the columns from "Always" to "Never."

Adapted from content posted on hbr.org on June 5, 2015, as "Quiz Yourself: Do You Lead with Emotional Intelligence?"

To calculate your score, as you finish each section count the checkmarks in each column and record the number in the "Total per column" line. Multiply your total score for each column by the number in the row below it, and record it in the row below that. Add this row together to get your total score for how you perceive yourself along each of the dimensions of EI.

Reflecting on your strengths and where you can improve is important, but don't stop there. Other people's perspectives matter too. After reviewing your scores, ask one or two trusted friends to evaluate you using the same statements, to learn what others see in you.

Annie McKee is a senior fellow at the University of Pennsylvania and the director of the PennCLO Executive Doctoral Program. She is the author of *Primal Leadership* (with Daniel Goleman and Richard Boyatzis), as well as *Resonant Leadership* and *Becoming a Resonant Leader*. Her new book, *How to Be Happy at Work*, is forthcoming from Harvard Business Review Press in September 2017.

HOW WOULD YOU DESCRIBE YOURSELF?

	ALWAYS	MOST OF THE TIME	FREQUENTLY	SOMETIMES	RARELY	NEVER
EMOTIONAL SELF-AWARENESS						
1 I can describe my emotions in the moment I experience them.						
2 I can describe my feelings in detail, beyond just "happy," "sad," "angry," and so on.						
3 I understand the reasons for my feelings.						
4 I understand how stress affects my mood and behavior.						
5 I understand my leadership strengths and weaknesses.						
Total per column						
Points per answer	x 5	x 4	x 3	x 2	x 1	x 0
Multiply the two rows above						
TOTAL SELF-AWARENESS SCORE (sum of the row above)						
POSITIVE OUTLOOK						
6 I'm optimistic in the face of challenging circumstances.						
7 I focus on opportunities rather than obstacles.						
8 I see people as good and well-intentioned.						
9 I look forward to the future.						
10 I feel hopeful.						
Total per column						
Points per answer	x 5	x 4	x 3	x 2	x 1	x 0
Multiply the two rows above						
TOTAL POSITIVE OUTLOOK SCORE (sum of the row above)						

HOW WOULD YOU DESCRIBE YOURSELF?

	ALWAYS	MOST OF THE TIME	FREQUENTLY	SOMETIMES	RARELY	NEVER
EMOTIONAL SELF-CONTROL						
11 I manage stress well.						
12 I'm calm in the face of pressure or emotional turmoil.						
13 I control my impulses.						
14 I use strong emotions, such as anger, fear, and joy, appropriately and for the good of others.						
15 I'm patient.						
Total per column						
Points per answer	x 5	x 4	x 3	x 2	x 1	x 0
Multiply the two rows above						
TOTAL EMOTIONAL SELF-CONTROL SCORE (sum of the row above)						
ADAPTABILITY						
16 I'm flexible when situations change unexpectedly.						
17 I'm adept at managing multiple, conflicting demands.						
18 I can easily adjust goals when circumstances change.						
19 I can shift my priorities quickly.						
20 I adapt easily when a situation is uncertain or ever-changing.						
Total per column						
Points per answer	x 5	x 4	x 3	x 2	x 1	x 0
Multiply the two rows above						
TOTAL ADAPTABILITY SCORE (sum of the row above)						

EMPATHY

		x 5	x 4	x 3	x 2	x 1	x 0
21	I strive to understand people's underlying feelings.						
22	My curiosity about others drives me to listen attentively to them.						
23	I try to understand why people behave the way they do.						
24	I readily understand others' viewpoints even when they are different from my own.						
25	I understand how other people's experiences affect their feelings, thoughts, and behavior.						
	Total per column						
	Points per answer	x 5	x 4	x 3	x 2	x 1	x 0
	Multiply the two rows above						
	TOTAL EMPATHY SCORE *(sum of the row above)*						

Self-Awareness: Understand Your Emotions, Know Your Behaviors

CHAPTER 3

You Can't Manage Emotions Without Knowing What They Really Are

by Art Markman

At this point, everybody knows emotional intelligence matters in the workplace. Yet there are two aspects of emotions that make it hard for people to exercise their emotional intelligence. First, most people are still not completely clear about what emotions actually are. Second, even when we understand emotions conceptually, it can still be hard to deal with our own emotional states.

To tackle the first problem: While in everyday speech, *emotion* and *feeling* are often used interchangeably,

Adapted from content posted on hbr.org on December 23, 2015 (product #H02KOK)

psychologists distinguish between them. Emotions are interpretations of feelings.

The feelings you have (what psychologists call *affect*) emerge from your motivational system. You generally feel good when you're succeeding at your goals and bad when you're not. The more deeply your motivational system is engaged with a situation, the stronger your feelings.

The motivational system, however, is not that well connected to the brain regions that help you to tell stories about the world. In order to make sense of what you're feeling, you use information about what's going on around you to help you translate those feelings into emotions—emotions help to guide your actions by giving you explicit feedback on how well you are currently achieving the goals the motivational system has engaged.

Often, that interpretation is easy. If you are crossing the street and suddenly have to leap out of the way of an oncoming car, it is clear that the strong negative feeling you are having is fear from nearly getting hit by the car. If a colleague compliments you on a job well done, it is obvious that the positive feeling you are having is pride.

But things are not always so clear. You might have a bad interaction with a family member before getting to work. As the day wears on, you may interpret your negative feelings as frustration with the project you're working on rather than lingering negative affect from the events of the morning.

Many people try to power through their negative feelings rather than attempting to understand them. But this is a lost opportunity. Emotions provide valuable information about the state of your motivational system. Ignoring them is like driving around lost, not only refusing to ask for directions but refusing to consult the map or the GPS—or even to look through the windshield. You will still be moving forward, but who knows where you will end up? Conversely, paying too much attention to your feelings is also bad. That's like staring at your road atlas without ever turning on the car: You can't get anywhere that way.

When you have negative feelings, slow down and pay some attention to *what* you are feeling and *why* you are feeling the way you are.

When you find yourself stressed, anxious, or angry, take five or 10 minutes for yourself during the day. Sit alone and breathe deeply. The deep breaths help to take some of the energy or arousal out of the feelings you are having. That can help you to think more clearly.

Then start to think about some of the events of your day. Pay attention to how those thoughts influence what you are feeling. Are there particular events that increase or decrease the intensity of those feelings?

You may not completely understand the source of your feelings the first time you do this. Over time, you will become more adept at paying attention to when and where you start to feel bad.

Of course, once you have figured out what's bothering you, it's time to plan a course of action. If you keep thinking about things that bother you, you run the risk of solving nothing while getting yourself more upset. Instead, use your knowledge about the source of the bad feeling to figure out how to deal with it.

Finally, if you're really upset about something, hold off on actually executing your plan until you have given yourself a chance to calm down. Responses that seemed like a good idea in the moment may seem less ideal to a cooler head.

Being willing to understand your feelings will have two benefits in the long term. First, it will help you to discover some of the aspects of your life that trigger negative feelings. That is useful, because you don't want to misinterpret your negative feelings and attribute them to something else. For example, you would like to be able to recognize when events in your personal life are spilling over into work and are causing you to feel badly about the work you do. Second, by understanding the sources of your own emotions, you will become more expert in understanding the people around you as well. We often ignore our own feelings—and then also ignore those of our colleagues.

Once you can better understand what emotions are and where your own emotions come from, you'll have a much better ability to practice emotional intelligence.

––––––––––––––

Art Markman, PhD, is the Annabel Irion Worsham Centennial Professor of Psychology and Marketing at the University of Texas at Austin and founding director of the program in the Human Dimensions of Organizations. He has written over 150 scholarly papers on topics including reasoning, decision making, and motivation. He is the author of several books including *Smart Thinking, Smart Change,* and *Habits of Leadership.*

CHAPTER 4

A Vocabulary for Your Emotions

by Susan David

Dealing effectively with emotions is a key leadership skill. And naming our emotions—what psychologists call *labeling*—is an important first step in dealing with them effectively. But it's harder than it sounds: Many of us struggle to identify what exactly we are feeling, and oftentimes the most obvious label isn't actually the most accurate.

There are a variety of reasons why this is so difficult: We've been trained to believe that strong emotions should be suppressed. We have certain (sometimes unspoken) societal and organizational rules against

---

Adapted from content posted on hbr.org on November 10, 2016, as "3 Ways to Better Understand Your Emotions" (product #H038KF)

expressing them. Or we've never learned a language to accurately describe our emotions. Consider these two examples:

Neena is in a meeting with Jared, and the whole time he has been saying things that make her want to explode. In addition to interrupting her at every turn, he's reminded everyone again *about that one project she worked on that failed. She's so angry.*

Mikhail gets home after a long day and sighs as he hangs up his coat. His wife asks if anything's wrong. "I'm just stressed," he says, pulling out his laptop to finish a report.

Anger and stress are two of the emotions we see most in the workplace—or at least, those are the terms we use for them most frequently. Yet they are often masks for deeper feelings that we could and should describe in more nuanced and precise ways, so that we develop greater levels of *emotional agility*, a critical capability that enables us to interact more successfully with ourselves and the world.

Yes, Neena may be mad, but what if she is also sad—sad that her project failed, and maybe also anxious that that failure is going to haunt her and her career? With Jared interrupting her so frequently, that anxiety feels increasingly justified. Why didn't the project work? And what's going to become of her job now? All of these emotions feed into her anger, but they are also separate feelings that she should identify and address.

And what if what's behind Mikhail's stress is the fact that he's just not sure he's in the right career? Long days used to be fun—why aren't they any more? He's surely stressed, but what's going on under that?

These questions open up a world of potential inquiry and answers for Neena and Mikhail. Like them, we need a more nuanced vocabulary for emotions, not just for the sake of being more precise, but because incorrectly diagnosing our emotions makes us respond incorrectly. If we think we need to attend to anger, we'll take a different approach than if we're handling disappointment or anxiety—or we might not address them at all. It's been shown that when people don't acknowledge and address their emotions, they display a lowered sense of well-being and more physical symptoms of stress, like headaches.[1] There is a high cost to avoiding our feelings.[2] On the flip side, having the right vocabulary allows us to see the real issue at hand—to take a messy experience, understand it more clearly, and build a roadmap to address the problem.[3]

Here are three ways to get a more accurate and precise sense of your emotions:

Broaden Your Emotional Vocabulary

Words matter. If you're experiencing a strong emotion, take a moment to consider what to call it. But don't stop there: Once you've identified it, try to come up with two more words that describe how you are feeling. You might be surprised at the breadth of your emotions—or that you've unearthed a deeper emotion buried beneath the more obvious one.

EXHIBIT 2

List of emotion terms

Angry	Sad	Anxious	Hurt	Embarrassed	Happy
Grumpy	Disappointed	Afraid	Jealous	Isolated	Thankful
Frustrated	Mournful	Stressed	Betrayed	Self-conscious	Trusting
Annoyed	Regretful	Vulnerable	Isolated	Lonely	Comfortable
Defensive	Depressed	Confused	Shocked	Inferior	Content
Spiteful	Paralyzed	Bewildered	Deprived	Guilty	Excited
Impatient	Pessimistic	Skeptical	Victimized	Ashamed	Relaxed
Disgusted	Tearful	Worried	Aggrieved	Repugnant	Relieved
Offended	Dismayed	Cautious	Tormented	Pathetic	Elated
Irritated	Disillusioned	Nervous	Abandoned	Confused	Confident

Exhibit 2 shows a vocabulary list of emotion terms; you can find much more by searching Google for any one of these.

It's equally important to do this with "positive" emotions as well as "negative" ones. Being able to say that you are *excited* about a new job (not just "I'm nervous") or *trusting* of a colleague (not just "He's nice"), for example, will help you set your intentions for the role or the relationship in a way that is more likely to lead to success down the road.

Consider the Intensity of the Emotion

We're apt to leap to basic descriptors like "angry" or "stressed" even when our feelings are far less extreme. I had a client, Ed (not his real name), who was struggling in his marriage; he frequently described his wife as "angry" and often got angry in return. But as the vocabulary chart suggests, every emotion comes in a variety of flavors. When we talked about other words for his wife's emotions, Ed saw that there were times that she was perhaps just annoyed or impatient. This insight completely changed their relationship, because he could suddenly see that she wasn't just angry all the time—and so could actually respond to her specific emotion and concern without getting angry himself. Similarly, it matters in your own self-assessment whether you are angry or just grumpy, mournful or just dismayed, elated or just pleased.

As you label your emotions, also rate them on a scale of 1–10. How deeply are you feeling the emotion? How urgent is it, or how strong? Does that make you choose a different set of words?

Write It Out

James Pennebaker has done 40 years of research into the links between writing and emotional processing. His experiments revealed that people who write about emotionally charged episodes experience a marked increase in their physical and mental well-being. Moreover, in a study of recently laid-off workers, he found that those who delved into their feelings of humiliation, anger, anxiety, and relationship difficulties were three times more likely to have been reemployed than those in control groups.

These experiments also revealed that over time those who wrote about their feelings began to develop insights into what those feelings meant (or didn't mean!), using phrases such as "I have learned . . ."; "It struck me that . . ."; "The reason that . . ."; "I now realize . . ."; and "I understand . . ." The process of writing allowed them to gain a new perspective on their emotions and to understand them and their implications more clearly.

Here's an exercise you can use to reflect through writing. You could do this every day, but it's particularly important when you're going through a tough time or a big transition, or if you're feeling emotional turmoil.

- Set a timer for 20 minutes.

- Using either a notebook or computer, write about your emotional experiences from the past week, month, or year.

- Don't worry about making it perfect or readable; go where your mind takes you.

- At the end, you don't have to save the document; the point is that those thoughts are now out of you and on the page.

You can also use these three approaches—broadening your vocabulary, noting the intensity of an emotion, and writing it out—when trying to better understand *another person's* emotions. As we saw with the example of Ed and his wife, we are just as likely to mislabel someone else's emotions as our own, with similarly complicating consequences. By understanding what they are feeling more precisely, you will be better equipped to respond in a constructive way.

Once you understand *what* you are feeling, then you can better address and learn from those more accurately described emotions. If Neena addresses the sadness and regret she feels in the wake of her failed project—as well as the anxiety about what it means for her career—that is more productive than trying to figure out how to deal with her anger at Jared. And if Mikhail can recognize his own career anxiety, he can start to craft a plan to build his future more deliberately—rather than simply miring himself in more of the same work when he gets home each night.

Susan David is a founder of the Harvard/McLean Institute of Coaching and is on faculty at Harvard University. She is author of *Emotional Agility* (Avery, 2016), based on the concept named by HBR as a Management Idea of the Year. As a speaker and adviser, David has worked with the senior leadership of hundreds of major organizations, including the United Nations, Ernst & Young, and the World Economic Forum. For more information, go to www.susandavid.com or follow her on Twitter @SusanDavid_PhD.

NOTES

1. Todd B. Kashdan, "Unpacking Emotion Differentiation: Transforming Unpleasant Experience by Perceiving Distinctions in Negativity," *Current Directions in Psychological Science* 24, no. 1 (2015).

2. Tori Rodriguez, "Negative Emotions Are Key to Well-Being," *Scientific American Mind*, May 1, 2013, https://www.scientific american.com/article/negative-emotions-key-well-being/.

3. Lisa Feldman Barrett et al., "Knowing What You're Feeling and Knowing What to Do About It: Mapping the Difference Between Emotion Differentiation and Emotion Regulation," *Cognition and Emotion* 15, no. 6 (2001): 713–724.

CHAPTER 5

Are You Sure You Show Respect?

by Christine Porath

For the last 20 years, I've studied the costs of incivility, as well as the benefits of civility. Across the board, I've found that civility pays. It enhances your influence and performance—and is positively associated with being perceived as a leader.[1]

Being respectful doesn't just benefit you, though; it benefits everyone around you. In a study of nearly 20,000 employees around the world (conducted with HBR), I found that when it comes to garnering commitment and engagement from employees, there's one thing that leaders need to demonstrate: respect. No other leadership behavior had a bigger effect on employees

Originally published on hbr.org on May 11, 2015, as "The Leadership Behavior That's Most Important to Employees" (product #H022CI)

across the outcomes we measured. Being treated with respect was more important to employees than recognition and appreciation, communicating an inspiring vision, providing useful feedback—or even opportunities for learning, growth, and development.

However, even when leaders know that showing respect is critical, many struggle to demonstrate it. If you're one of those leaders, consider the following steps:

Ask for focused feedback on your best behaviors

This technique, originated by researcher Laura Roberts and colleagues, will help you see your most respectful self.[2] Collect feedback via email from about 10 people (coworkers, friends, family). Ask each for positive examples of your best behavior. When and how have they seen you treat people well? After compiling the feedback, try to organize the data by summarizing and categorizing it into themes. For example, create a table with columns for commonality, examples (of the behavior), and your thoughts. You might also use Wordle.net to identify themes (you'll also get a colorful picture that can serve as a reminder of you at your best, most civil self). Then look for patterns: When, where, how, with whom are you at your best? Use your insights to reinforce what you're doing well. Be mindful of additional opportunities to be your best civil self. Leverage your interpersonal strengths.

Discover your shortcomings

Gather candid feedback from your colleagues and friends not only on what you're doing that conveys respect, but also on how you can improve. Specifically, what are your shortcomings? Identify a couple of trusted colleagues who have the best intentions for you and your organization. These are folks who you believe will provide direct and honest feedback. Ask for their views about how you treat other people. What do you do well? What could you do better? Listen carefully.

Consider the actions of Lieutenant Christopher Manning, a naval intelligence officer at the Pentagon, who has systematized ways to get continuous feedback from his direct reports. He expanded the scope of anonymous feedback surveys to include not only how he could improve the organization and himself as a leader, but also his team members' personal happiness (e.g., including how supported people felt by him), and work-life balance. He also instituted an anonymous comment box and encouraged an open-door policy. He even provides incentives for the most insightful critiques, such as the chance to attend a course or conference of interest, extra time off, and public recognition. And he meets one-on-one with his direct reports frequently. The regular feedback from these sources has helped him hone his skills. The bonus: He's found that those who report to him are more engaged and respect him more.

If you don't feel comfortable soliciting the feedback of your entire team, you can also ask a trusted direct report to gather feedback within the organization about whether you (the leader) consistently demonstrate civility, and what situations may trigger uncivil behavior.

Work with a coach

Coaches can uncover potential weaknesses through surveying and interviewing those with whom you work; they can also shadow you at meetings and events to pick up on subtleties including nonverbal behavior. A skilled coach may unearth some of the underlying assumptions, experiences, and personal qualities that make one prone to uncivil behavior.

Ask, specifically, how you can improve

Once you have clarity on which behaviors you want to improve, gather information from others about *how* best to go about this. This "feedforward" method, originated by author Marshall Goldsmith, is a terrific way to gather specific ideas for improving your behavior. The process consists of five steps:

1. Describe your goal clearly and simply to anyone you know.

2. Ask for two suggestions. Encourage creative ideas.

3. Listen carefully. Write the suggestions down.

4. Respond with "thank you." Nothing more. No excuses or defensiveness.

5. Repeat by asking additional people.

Enlist your team in keeping you accountable

Choose one change that could improve your behavior and then experiment, asking your team to help you by letting you know when they see improvement. For example, after a meeting, ask your team if they saw an improvement in the behavior that you're working on. What was the impact?

Here's an example: A woman I know of—let's call her Karen—enlisted her team to help her change a specific behavior. The team had grown increasingly frustrated by her inability to listen and empower them. While she was highly intelligent, she was constantly interrupting people in meetings and taking over initial ideas before they could even be presented. Karen worked with a coach to develop a technique to avoid this pattern—in this case, tapping her toe instead of interrupting someone. (Other coaches have developed similar techniques, such as counting to 10.) She informed her team that she was working on the behavior, and after a couple of days of meetings, she checked in with them on her progress. This helped establish a norm for more open dialogue—and a shared sense that the team members could count on each other to support their own development.

Make time for reflection

Keep a journal to provide insight into when/where/why you are your best and when you are uncivil. Identify situations that cause you to lose your temper. A leader I worked with named Monica noticed that she was far more curt in the late afternoon. She began her days before 5:00 a.m. By the time late afternoon hit, she was tired and was less emotionally attuned. She was brusque in conversations and less civil in email. Before she started journaling and reflecting on her day, Monica was unaware of the effect of time of day—and her energy management—on her demeanor. Now she is much more mindful of her behavior. For challenging situations such as conflict, people who trigger her, and communication that requires tact, she waits until the following morning to respond.

Consider tracking your own energy through the day via an energy audit tool, such as "Energy Audit—Awareness and Action," which is available from the University of Michigan.[3] Reflection helps you identify strategies to maintain composure and be your best, most civil self. After adopting some of the improvement strategies, do you see a decrease in incivility, or an increase in civility? Track yourself and review progress on a regular basis (e.g., weekly or monthly).

The path toward building greater self-awareness and treating people more respectfully at work doesn't have to be walked alone. While you're working to improve your own behavior, encourage your team members to do the same. Have an open discussion with your team about what you and your teammates do or say that conveys respect. How or when are you and your teammates less than civil to each other? What could you do or say better? Discuss what the team will gain by being more respectful of each other. As the entire team develops norms, hold one another accountable for them. Consider yourselves coaches that are helping to improve both individual and team performance.

The key to mastering civility begins with improving your self-awareness. Armed with this information, you can begin tweaking your behavior to enhance your influence and effectiveness. Small acts can have big returns. Your civility will cascade throughout your organization, with benefits to you—and your organization.

Christine Porath is an associate professor of management at Georgetown University, the author of *Mastering Civility: A Manifesto for the Workplace* (Grand Central Publishing, forthcoming), and a coauthor of *The Cost of Bad Behavior* (Portfolio, 2009).

NOTES

1. Christine L. Porath et al., "The Effects of Civility on Advice, Leadership, and Performance," *Journal of Applied Psychology* 100 no. 5, (September 2015): 1527–1541.

2. Center for Positive Organizations, "Reflected Best Self Exercise," http://positiveorgs.bus.umich.edu/cpo-tools/reflected-best-self -exercise-2nd-edition/.

3. The energy audit is available at http://positiveorgs.bus.umich .edu/wp-content/uploads/GrantSpreitzer-EnergyAudit.pdf.

Manage Your Emotions

CHAPTER 6

Make Your Emotions Work for You

by Susan David

We often hear tips and tricks for helping us to "control" our emotions, but that's the wrong idea. Strong emotions aren't bad; they don't need to be pushed down or controlled; they are, in fact, data. Our emotions evolved as a signaling system, a way to help us communicate with each other and to better understand ourselves. What we need to do is learn to develop *emotional agility*, the capacity to mine even the most difficult emotions for data that can help us make better decisions.

Adapted from content posted on hbr.org on November 28, 2016, as "How to Manage Your Emotions Without Fighting Them" (product #H038NO)

What's the Function of the Emotion?

To make the most of that data, ask yourself what the *function* of your emotion is. What is it telling you? What is it trying to signal?

Consider the example of Mikhail, who found himself in a perpetual cycle of stress because of the never-ending onslaught of tasks at work. As he more precisely defined his emotions, he realized what he was feeling wasn't just stress: he felt a more general dissatisfaction with his work, disappointment in some of his career choices, and anxiety about what the future held for him. Once Mikhail recognized and accepted these emotions, he was able to see what they were signaling to him: He had started to question whether he was on the right career path.

This revelation meant that instead of tackling a productivity problem by becoming more disciplined about prioritizing his tasks or saying no to extra work, Mikhail was able to do something much more appropriate and constructive. He began working with a career coach. By examining what his emotions were telling him, rather than pushing them away or focusing on the wrong problem, he learned something new about himself and was eventually able to find a new career path where he was just as busy—but felt much less stressed.

Our emotions can teach us valuable lessons. Let them shine a light on what you want to change, how you want to act in the future, or what is valuable to you.

Is Your Reaction Aligned with Your Values?

Our emotions can also help us understand our deepest values. They can often signal what is more important to us: You feel love for your family. You feel ambition at work and appreciate achievement and self-worth. You feel fulfilled when you've been able to help a direct report achieve their goals. You feel peace and satisfaction on a mountain summit. It's far better to focus on these deeper values rather than your immediate emotions, which can spur poor decisions.

Let's say that you need to give some difficult feedback to one of your direct reports. You're anxious about the conversation and you've been putting it off (which just makes you more anxious). In examining your emotions, you realize that one of the values behind your procrastination is fairness. She's a strong employee, and you just don't want to be unfair to her. So, you ask yourself: How does having or not having the conversation either bring you toward or move you away from your value of fairness? Looking at the situation in this light, you can see that giving her the feedback and helping her to succeed is actually *more* fair to her—and to your whole team—than caving to your anxieties. You've been able to unhook yourself from the thrall of your immediate emotions and make a better choice that is true to the values that underlie them.

This kind of thinking can help you avoid situations in which you do something that makes you feel good in the short term but doesn't align with your values in the long term. Avoiding a conversation is a typical example, but there are many others: brashly telling someone off for getting on your nerves when you value compassion; sticking with a comfortable job that doesn't align with your dream of starting a business when you value growth; criticizing yourself for the smallest things when you really value self-affirmation.

Managing emotions isn't just doing away with them; it's putting strategies in place that let you use them effectively rather than letting them govern your behaviors and actions. Your emotions are your natural guidance system—and they are more effective when you don't try to fight them.

––––––––––––

Susan David is a founder of the Harvard/McLean Institute of Coaching and is on faculty at Harvard University. She is author of *Emotional Agility* (Avery, 2016), based on the concept named by HBR as a Management Idea of the Year. As a speaker and adviser, David has worked with the senior leadership of hundreds of major organizations, including the United Nations, Ernst & Young, and the World Economic Forum. For more information, go to www.susandavid.com or follow her on Twitter @SusanDavid_PhD.

CHAPTER 7

Defuse a Challenging Interaction

Conflicts stir up many emotions, especially negative thoughts and feelings. To successfully manage these disagreements in the moment, you need to address your own emotions as well as those of the other person.

Reframe Negative Thoughts

During difficult interactions, you may begin to question your perceptions about yourself. For example, suppose a direct report says, "I didn't attend the meeting because I didn't think you valued my ideas." In response, you

Adapted from "Address Emotions" in the Harvard ManageMentor topic "Difficult Interactions" (Harvard Business Publishing, 2016, electronic)

wonder to yourself, "Maybe I'm not a competent manager after all."

For many people, the sense that their self-image is being challenged creates intense emotions. These feelings can become overwhelming, making it virtually impossible to converse productively about any subject. To experience—and then let go of—difficult feelings:

- **Focus on the other person's intentions and on the facts.** If you discover that your employee had legitimate reasons for not showing up at a weekly meeting, your annoyance may fade away.

- **Examine your contributions to the problem.** If you realize that you've accidentally advised an employee to focus on an unnecessary task, your frustration may dissipate.

- **Question your assumptions.** If you find your belief that a colleague doesn't value product quality is mistaken, you may feel less anger over her tendency to take shortcuts.

Your goal in reframing negative thoughts is to be able to express your complete range of emotions without judging or blaming the other person.

Neutralize Unproductive Behaviors

Although you can work to manage your own reactions, you can't control those of the other person in the conflict. Try the techniques in exhibit 3 for dealing with unproductive behaviors:

EXHIBIT 3

Tackling unproductive behaviors

If the other person . . .	Try to . . .
Is aggressive and disrespectful	• Command respect by remaining calm. • Interrupt verbal attacks by repeating the person's name. • Communicate your bottom line: "When you're ready to speak to me with respect, I will take all the time you want to discuss this."
Doesn't listen to your side	• Go into the conversation prepared to support your own perceptions and ideas. • Redirect the person to your idea or information with phrases such as "I was just wondering . . . " "Bear with me a minute," or "What do you suppose . . . ?" • Acknowledge that the person possesses valuable knowledge, too.
Has an explosive outburst	• Take a break and then continue the conversation. • Get the person's attention by waving your arms and calling their name loudly enough to be heard. • Express genuine concern for the person: "Joe, nobody should have to feel this way! I want to help."
Is uncommunicative	• Schedule plenty of time for the person to respond to your ideas and questions. • Ask open-ended questions: "What are you thinking?" "How do you want to proceed?" "Where should we go from here?" • Gaze expectantly at the person for a longer-than-usual period of time after making a comment or asking a question.
Assumes that the situation can't get better	• Give the person time to consider your plan and get back to you. • Bring up and address the negative aspects of an idea before the other person does.

CHAPTER 8

Stay Grounded in Stressful Moments

by Leah Weiss

Mindfulness should be as much a physical practice as it is a mental one. Given its name, you might think mindfulness is something you do only with your mind. In fact, lots of research, including my own, has shown that paying attention to our bodies is often an easy way into mindfulness and helps us reduce stress while it's happening.

This may seem counterintuitive because when our mind is overwhelmed, our body is often the last thing we're thinking about. If we notice our bodies at all in moments of stress, most likely it is as they interrupt our

---

Adapted from content posted on hbr.org on November 18, 2016, as "A Simple Way to Stay Grounded in Stressful Moments" (product #H039WF)

normal activities: carpal tunnel syndrome, back pain, breast pumping, dental appointments, sore feet, sick days, or simply the routine hunger that forces us to stop what we're doing multiple times a day and eat. Yet if we focus our attention on our bodies, they can be our anchor in what's happening right now, even if the sensations are unpleasant.

This is how anchoring works: We bring our attention into our bodies, noticing—rather than avoiding—the tension, circulation, pain, pleasure, or just neutral physical experience of, say, our right shoulder or the arch of our left foot. This practice helps us snap back to reality. In fact, our bodies are the quickest, surest way back to the present moment when our minds are lost in rehashing the past or rehearsing the future.

We cause ourselves a lot of unnecessary suffering when our minds aren't paying attention. The amygdala, located in the brain's medial temporal lobe, is the part of the brain that detects and processes fear. When our amygdala is activated by a situation that is interpreted as a potential threat, even if we are just reading an unpleasant email, it initiates physiological changes such as increased muscle tension and accelerated breathing. This association becomes so strong that we take the body's reaction as evidence of danger, just as Pavlov's dogs took the sound of the bell as evidence of dinner. As a result, a vicious cycle can develop wherein the increased muscle tension and rapid breathing caused by an activated amygdala further activates the amygdala. Thankfully, we can use anchoring to break out of it.

One of my students who was working on a startup business used to panic before meeting with potential venture capitalists. His mind would spin with fears of the worst outcomes: his pitch rejected, his business idea exposed as worthless. Once he learned to tune in to his body, to use a brief minute to anchor by taking a few breaths and feeling his feet on the ground, he calmed down and became poised to have much better conversations. Here are some simple, effective anchoring practices you can use:

- **Take a single breath.** It takes just one intentional breath to change our perspective. A single breath gives you a break from the mind's chatter and a chance for your body to regulate after amping up in response to a perceived threat. Most of the time, when you're in distress, you're in the middle of telling yourself a story and you fully believe it. A breath can take you out of the story, making you less gullible. You can follow the breath into your body, where you gain just enough distance to judge whether your head is with you (in line with your current intentions and greater purpose) or against you, and then consciously choose which way you want to go.

- **Pay attention to emotions.** Another reason to anchor in your body is that it's where you feel your emotions, which are important to acknowledge even if they may seem like a liability, especially at work. I've studied the downsides of emotional suppression and I can assure you—it's not beneficial.[1]

It's paradoxical, but nonjudgmentally engaging with negative emotions *negatively* correlates with negative emotions and mood disorder. In other words, if you acknowledge and recognize unpleasant emotions, they have less power to cause you distress. In one study, participants wrote every day for four days about either a traumatic experience or a neutral event.[2] Those who wrote about trauma made fewer health center visits in the following six months than those who wrote about a neutral event. When you pay attention to your body, you can catch emotional information upstream, before it hijacks your whole system—once it does, it's too late to use it to your advantage.

- **Remember that your colleagues have bodies too.** Annoyed with your boss? Think you can't last another day with an impossible colleague? If you let it, your body can connect you to other people— even difficult ones—since the body is a major part of what we have in common. This sounds obvious, but the implications are profound. Our bodies and the pleasure and pain that come with them—their attendant aches and illnesses, their needs and indignities, the impossibility of choosing the one we want, the fear of losing it someday, and the ways we fight our bodies or pretend they don't exist—are shared experiences. When you ignore your body (or try to), you miss out on a fundamental part of what we have in common. The empathy gained from this awareness helps you to have productive professional relationships, rather than suffering from ongoing frustration and pain.

- **Magnify little pleasures.** Don't underestimate the joy of taking that first sip of afternoon coffee. It's human nature to notice pain more than pleasure, but with reminders and practice you can experience joy throughout the day in the simple, reliable pleasures of having a body. It might be from sitting when you've been standing for too long, or standing up and stretching when you've been sitting; holding a new pen with a particularly cushy, ergonomic grip; laughing hard when something's funny; eating when you're hungry; the relative quiet of the office after a morning with screaming kids; slipping out of uncomfortable shoes under your desk. Every day, no matter how lousy, affords countless opportunities like these to feel good. Recently, I had a meeting at the VA hospital in Palo Alto and came across two veterans as I was walking. They were sitting in front of the building, both in wheelchairs. One man leaned over to his companion and said, "Well, it's great that we can move our hands." The other responded, "Yes, you are right. That is great!" Their perspective provides a powerful reminder that most of us can, if we choose, find within our daily routine a small joy worthy of being celebrated.

Stress is an inevitable aspect of our lives at work, but you don't need elaborate practices or escape mechanisms to engage with it. You simply need to have the wherewithal to ground yourself in a physical sensation, to anchor and come back to reality. You need only a brief moment to tap your feet on the ground and be reminded that you have a reliable and ever-present instrument to mitigate your stress. And, it just so happens, you were born with it.

———————

Leah Weiss is a teacher, writer, and researcher at Stanford Graduate School of Business, the Director of Education at HopeLab, and the author of the forthcoming book *Heart at Work*.

NOTES

1. Debora Cutuli, "Cognitive Reappraisal and Expressive Suppression Strategies Role in the Emotion Regulation: An Overview on Their Modulatory Effects and Neural Correlates," *Frontiers in Systems Neuroscience*, September 19, 2014; Andrea Hermann et al., "Brain Structural Basis of Cognitive Reappraisal and Expressive Suppression," *Social Cognitive and Effective Neuroscience* 9, no. 9 (September 2014): 1435–1442.; and Sally Moore et al., "Are Expressive Suppression and Cognitive Reappraisal Associated with Stress-Related Symptoms?" *Behaviour Research and Therapy* 46, no. 9 (September 2008): 993–1000

2. James J. Gross, ed., *Handbook of Emotion Regulation*, 2nd edition. New York: The Guilford Press, 2014.

CHAPTER 9

Recovering from an Emotional Outburst

by Susan David

It happens—we all get emotional at work. You might scream, or cry, or pound the table and stamp your feet. This is not ideal office behavior, of course, and there are ramifications to these outbursts, but they don't have to be career-killers either. If you take a close look at what happened, why you acted the way you did, and take steps to remedy the situation, you can turn an outburst into an opportunity.

Adapted from content posted on hbr.org on May 8, 2015, as "Recovering from an Emotional Outburst at Work" (product #H022A3)

If you tend to suppress your emotions, you're likely to just ignore your tantrum and move on. If you are prone to ruminating over your mistakes, you'll overthink your outburst and beat yourself up about it.

Neither of these strategies is productive; they don't help you solve the problem *or* promote your own well-being. Instead, treat your outburst for what it is: data. A key emotional intelligence skill is being able to manage your emotion, but you can't manage what you can't recognize and understand. So first, be open to emotions. What was I feeling here? Emotions are signals, beacons that show you that you care about something.

To *recognize* your emotions, you have to be able to differentiate between feelings—sadness, anger, frustration (see chapter 4 in this guide). In many work environments, people suffer from what psychologists call *alexithymia*—a dispositional difficulty in accurately labeling and expressing what they're feeling. These people tend to be vague about their emotions. So a manager will say to herself, for example, "Gee, I yelled because I was really stressed out." But that gives her no information about what was really going on.

Once you've recognized the emotion—fear, disappointment, anger—your next step is to *understand* what, exactly, caused it: "Why is it that I reacted in this particular way?" "What was happening in this situation that I found upsetting?" "What values of mine may have been transgressed or challenged?" For example, maybe you lost it and screamed at a colleague when you found out that your project was cut. If you dig deeper, you may find that it wasn't exactly about the project but rather how the decision was made—that you didn't feel it was made fairly.

The research on emotions shows that there are general triggers that you should be aware of.[1] When your outburst is anger—yelling, stomping your feet—it's typically because you're frustrated or feel thwarted. You've been stopped from doing something that's important to you. When you feel sadness or cry, it's usually because of a loss. Acting out on anxiety is prompted by a sense of threat. It's helpful to think about these universal triggers, and then ask, "What is it specifically that was important to me in this situation?"

Once you've recognized how you feel, and why you feel it, you can focus on what to do to make things better—to *manage* the situation. It goes without saying that you should apologize if you yelled or lost your cool, but that's not enough. Your goal isn't just to repair the relationship, but to strengthen it.

After you've calmed down and you return to your team the following day or week, instead of saying, "Gee, I'm so sorry about what I did; now let's move on," address what really happened for you. You might say something like, "I got really mad and I'm not proud of my behavior. I've been thinking long and hard about what it was that I found so upsetting and I've realized that my sense of fairness was challenged because of how the defunding decisions were made."

There's research that shows that when you appropriately disclose your emotions in this way, people are more likely to treat you with compassion and forgiveness than if you had just offered an apology.[2] From there you start a shared conversation about what's important to each of you and how you can work better together.

No one wants to earn a reputation as a crier or a screamer at work. Instead of running and hiding or wallowing in self-pity when you've lost it, bring a good dose of compassion and curiosity to the situation. To be kind and compassionate toward yourself—especially in the moments you are least proud of—is not the same as letting yourself off the hook. In fact, studies show that people who are self-compassionate are much more likely to hold themselves to high standards and work to make things right.[3] And treating yourself that way is more likely to inspire others to do the same.

Susan David is a founder of the Harvard/McLean Institute of Coaching and is on faculty at Harvard University. She is author of *Emotional Agility* (Avery, 2016), based on the concept named by HBR as a Management Idea of the Year. As a speaker and adviser, David has worked with the senior leadership of hundreds of major organizations, including the United Nations, Ernst & Young, and the World Economic Forum. For more information, go to www.susandavid.com or follow her on Twitter @SusanDavid_PhD.

NOTES

1. R. S. Lazarus, "From Psychological Stress to Emotions: A History of Changing Outlooks," *Annual Review of Psychology* 44 (1993): 1–22.

2. James J. Gross, "Emotion Regulation: Affective, Cognitive, and Social Consequences," *Psychophysiology* 39 (2002): 281–291.

3. Kristin D. Neff, "Self-Compassion, Self-Esteem, and Well-Being," *Social and Personality Psychology Compass* 5, no. 1 (2011): 1–12.

Everyday Emotional Intelligence

CHAPTER 10

Writing Resonant Emails

by Andrew Brodsky

Imagine sending a detailed question to your boss and getting a one-word response: "No." Is she angry? Offended by your email? Or just very busy? When I conduct research with organizations on the topic of communication, one of the most common themes raised by both employees and managers is the challenge of trying to communicate emotional or sensitive issues over email. Email, of course, lacks most normal cues for relaying emotion, such as tone of voice and facial expressions.

But in many cases, using email is simply unavoidable. So how can you balance the need to communicate with

Adapted from content posted on hbr.org on April 23, 2013, as "The Do's and Don'ts of Work Email" (product #H020WK)

avoiding the potential pitfalls of using emotion in email? Here are three concrete, research-based recommendations:

Understand what drives how emails are interpreted

It is clear that people often misinterpret emotion in email, but what drives the direction of the misinterpretation? For one, people infuse their emotional expectations into how they read messages, regardless of the sender's actual intent.[1] Consider the email, *"Good job on the current draft, but I think we can continue to improve it."* Coming from a peer, this email will seem very collaborative; coming from a supervisor, it may seem critical.

In addition to relative position (emails from people high in power tend to be perceived as more negative), there are other contextual factors to consider: the length of a relationship (emails from people we know well tend to be perceived as less negative), the emotional history of the relationship, and the individual's personality (negative people tend to perceive messages as more negative).

The first step in avoiding miscommunication is to try to stand in the recipient's shoes, and imagine how they are likely to interpret your message. Doing so can help you to prevent misunderstandings before they ever occur.

Mimic behaviors

What is the best way to convey emotions via email? Emoticons? Word choice? Exclamation points? There is no single correct answer; the proper cues will vary based on the context. For instance, you likely wouldn't want to send a smiley face emoticon to a client organization that is known for having a very formal culture. Alternatively, you wouldn't want to send an overly formal email to a very close colleague.

One strategy that has been found to be very effective across settings is to engage in behavioral mimicry—using emoticons, word-choice, and slang/jargon in a similar manner to the person with whom you are communicating. In a set of studies of American, Dutch, and Thai negotiators, using behavioral mimicry in the early stages of text-based chat negotiations increased individual outcomes by 30%. This process of mimicry increases trust because people tend to feel an affinity toward those who act similarly to them.[2]

State your emotions

While mimicking behaviors can be effective, it is still a rather subtle strategy that leaves the potential for emotional ambiguity. The simplest solution to avoid any confusion is to just explicitly state the emotion that you want to relay in your email.

One excellent example of how this works comes from a media organization I recently worked with. I asked employees for an email that they felt was written very poorly, and one employee provided me with the following message from a manager:

The intro of the commercial needs to be redone. I'm sure that's the client's doing and you will handle it :). Warm Regards, [Manager's Name].

To me as an outsider (and I'm guessing to the manager as well), this email seemed well crafted to avoid offending the employee. However, the employee felt differently and explained: "She knows perfectly well that I made the terrible intro, and she was saying, 'Well, I'm sure the client made that segment and that you will tackle it,' and then she put a little smiley face at the end. So overall, a condescendingly nasty tone."

If the manager had avoided subtlety and stated her meaning directly, there might have been less room for interpretation. For example, what if she had written:

I am very happy with your work so far. I think the intro could be improved, though; would you mind giving it another shot?

The employee would have had far less ambiguity to fill in with her own emotional expectations.

Yet people rarely state their intended emotions, even when the stakes are high. Research from NYU has shown that many people are overconfident in their ability to accurately relay emotions when it comes to email.[3] It may seem obvious to the message sender that a coworker who never takes sick days will realize a comment about them leaving early is humorous rather than serious. However, that coworker might be particularly concerned about being seen as lazy and will feel hurt or offended.

Given the constantly evolving nature of organizational communication, there is still a lot to learn about effective email use. However, there are some clear areas where we can improve. In reality, we all have the same flaw: We tend to be overly focused on ourselves and our own goals, while failing to amply account for other people's perspectives. Using these methods for bridging your and your email recipient's perspectives, by both increasing message clarity and building trust, will help you to ensure effective communication.

Andrew Brodsky is a PhD candidate in organizational behavior at Harvard Business School.

NOTES

1. Kristin Byron, "Carrying Too Heavy a Load? The Communication and Miscommunication of Emotion by Email," *Academy of Management Review* 33, no. 2 (April 2008): 309–327.

2. William W. Maddux et al., "Chameleons Bake Bigger Pies and Take Bigger Pieces: Strategy Behavioral Mimicry Facilitates Negotiation Outcomes," *Journal of Experimental Social Psychology* 44, no. 2 (March 2008): 461–468; and Roderick I. Swaab et al., "Early Words That Work: When and How Virtual Linguistic Mimicry Facilitates Negotiation Outcomes," *Journal of Experimental Psychology* 47, no. 3 (May 2011): 616–621.

3. Justin Kruger et al., "Egocentrism Over E-mail: Can We Communicate as Well as We Think?" *Journal of Personality and Social Psychology* 89, no. 6 (December 2005): 925–936.

CHAPTER 11

Running Powerful Meetings

by Annie McKee

Yes, we all hate meetings. Yes, they are usually a waste of time. And yes, they're here to stay. So it's your responsibility as a leader to make them better. This doesn't mean just making them shorter, more efficient, and more organized. People need to enjoy them and—dare I say it—have fun.

So how do we fix meetings so they are more enjoyable and produce more positive feelings? Sure, invite the right people, create better agendas, and be better prepared. Those are baseline fixes. But if you really want to improve how people work together at meetings, you'll need to rely on—and maybe develop—a couple of key

Adapted from content posted on hbr.org on March 23, 2015, as "Empathy Is Key to a Great Meeting" (product #H01YDY)

emotional intelligence competencies: empathy and emotional self-management.

Why empathy? Empathy is a competency that allows you to read people. Who is supporting whom? Who is pissed off, and who is coasting? Where is the resistance? This isn't as easy as it seems. Sometimes, the smartest resisters often look like supporters, but they're not supportive at all. They're smart, sneaky idea killers.

Carefully reading people will also help you understand the major and often hidden conflicts in the group. Hint: These conflicts probably have nothing to do with the topics discussed or decisions being made at the meeting. They are far more likely to be linked to very human dynamics like who is allowed to influence whom (headquarters versus the field, expats versus local nationals) and power dynamics between genders and among people of various races.

Empathy lets you see and manage these power dynamics. Many of us would like to think that these sorts of concerns—and office politics in general—are beneath us, unimportant, or just for those Machiavellian folks we all dislike. Realistically, though, power is hugely important in groups because it is the real currency in most organizations. And it plays out in meetings. Learning to read how the flow of power is moving and shifting can help you lead the meeting—and everything else.

Keep in mind that employing empathy will help you understand how people are responding to *you*. As a leader you may be the most powerful person at the meeting. Some people, the dependent types, will defer at every turn. That feels good, for a minute. Carry on that way, and you're likely to create a dependent group—or one that is polarized between those who will do anything you want and those who will not.

This is where emotional self-management comes in, for a couple of reasons. First, take a look at the dependent folks in your meetings. Again, it can feel really good to have people admire you and agree with your every word. In fact, this can be a huge relief in our conflict-ridden organizations. But again, if you don't manage your response, you will make group dynamics worse. You will also look like a fool. Others are reading the group, too, and they will rightly read that you like it when people go along with you. They will see that you are falling prey to your own ego or to those who want to please or manipulate you.

Second, strong emotions set the tone for the entire group. We take our cue from one another about how to feel about what's going on around us. Are we in danger? Is there cause for celebration? Should we be fed up and cynical or hopeful and committed? Here's why this matters in meetings: If you, as a leader, effectively project out your more positive emotions, such as hope and enthusiasm, others will "mirror" these feelings and the general tone of the group will be marked by optimism and a sense of "we're in this together, and we can do it."[1] And there is a strong neurological link between feelings and cognition. We think more clearly and more creatively when our feelings are largely positive and when we are appropriately challenged, as Mihaly Csikszentmihalyi wrote in his classic *Creativity: Flow and the Psychology of Discovery and Invention.*

The other side of the coin is obvious. Your negative emotions are also contagious, and they are almost always destructive if unchecked and unmanaged. Express anger, contempt, or disrespect, and you will definitely push people into fight mode—individually and collectively. Express disdain, and you'll alienate people far beyond the end of the meeting. And it doesn't matter who you feel this way about. All it takes is for people to see it, and they will catch it—and worry that next time your target will be them.

This is not to say that all positive emotions are good all the time or that you should never express negative emotions. The point is that the leader's emotions are highly infectious. Know this and manage your feelings accordingly to create the kind of environment where people can work together to make decisions and get things done.

It may go without saying, but you can't do any of this with your phone on. As Daniel Goleman shares in his book *Focus: The Hidden Driver of Excellence*, we are not nearly as good at multitasking as we think we are. Actually we stink at it. So turn it off and pay attention to the people you are with today.

In the end, it's your job to make sure people leave your meeting feeling pretty good about what's happened, their contributions, and you as the leader. Empathy allows you to read what's going on, and self-management helps you move the group to a mood that supports getting things done—and happiness.

Annie McKee is a senior fellow at the University of Pennsylvania and the director of the PennCLO Executive Doctoral Program. She is the author of *Primal Leadership* (with Daniel Goleman and Richard Boyatzis), as well as *Resonant Leadership* and *Becoming a Resonant Leader*. Her new book, *How to Be Happy at Work*, is forthcoming from Harvard Business Review Press in September 2017.

NOTE

1. V. Ramachandran, "The Neurons That Shaped Civilization," TED talk, November 2009, https://www.ted.com/talks/vs_rama chandran_the_neurons_that_shaped_civilization?language=en.

CHAPTER 12

Giving Difficult Feedback

by Monique Valcour

Over the years, I've asked hundreds of executive students what skills they believe are essential for leaders. "The ability to give tough feedback" comes up frequently. But what exactly is "tough feedback"? The phrase connotes bad news, like when you have to tell a team member that they've screwed up on something important. "Tough" also signifies the way we think we need to be when giving negative feedback: firm, resolute, and unyielding.

But "tough" also points to the discomfort some of us experience when giving negative feedback, and to the challenge of doing so in a way that motivates change

---

Adapted from content posted on hbr.org on August 11, 2015, as "How to Give Tough Feedback That Helps People Grow" (product #H029QB)

instead of making the other person feel defensive. Managers fall into a number of common traps when offering feedback. We might be angry at an employee and use the conversation to blow off steam rather than to coach. Or we may delay giving needed feedback because we anticipate that the employee will become argumentative and refuse to accept responsibility. We might try surrounding negative feedback with positive feedback, like disguising a bitter-tasting pill in a spoonful of honey. But this approach is misguided, because we don't want the negative feedback to slip by unnoticed in the honey. Instead, it's essential to create conditions in which the receiver can take in feedback, reflect on it, and learn from it.

To get a feel for what this looks like in practice, I juxtapose two feedback conversations that occurred following a workplace conflict. MJ Paulitz, a physical therapist in the Pacific Northwest, was treating a hospital patient one day when a fellow staff member paged her. Following procedure, she excused herself and stepped out of the treatment room to respond to the page. The colleague who sent it didn't answer her phone when MJ called, nor had she left a message describing the situation that warranted the page. This happened two more times during the same treatment session. The third time she left her patient to respond to the page, MJ lost her cool and left an angry voicemail message for her colleague. Upset upon hearing the message, the staff member reported it to their supervisor as abusive.

MJ's first feedback session took place in her supervisor's office. She recalls, "When I went into his office, he had already decided that I was the person at fault, he had all the information he needed, and he wasn't interested in hearing my side of the story. He did not address the three times she pulled me out of patient care. He did not acknowledge that that might have been the fuse that set me off." Her supervisor referred MJ to the human resources department for corrective action. She left seething with a sense of injustice.

MJ describes the subsequent feedback conversation with human resources as transformative. "The woman in HR could see that I had a lot of just-under-the-surface feelings, and she acknowledged them. The way she did it was genius: She eased into it. She didn't make me go first. Instead, she said, 'I can only imagine what you're feeling right now. Here you are in my office, in corrective action. If it were me, I might be feeling angry, frustrated, embarrassed . . . Are any of these true for you?' That made a huge difference."

With trust established, MJ was ready to take responsibility for her behavior and commit to changing it. Next the HR person said, "Now let's talk about how you reacted to those feelings in the moment." She created a space that opened up a genuine dialogue.

The subsequent conversation created powerful learning that has stuck with MJ to this day:

> Oftentimes, when we're feeling a strong emotion, we go down what the HR person called a "cowpath," because it's well worn, very narrow, and always leads to the same place. Let's say you're angry. What do you do?

You blow up. It's okay that you feel those things; it's just not okay to blow up. She asked me to think about what I could do to get on a different path.

The feedback from the HR person helped me learn to find the space between what I'm feeling and the next thing that slides out of my mouth. She gave me the opportunity to grow internally. What made it work was establishing a safe space, trust, and rapport, and then getting down to "you need to change"—rather than starting with "you need to change," which is what my supervisor did. I did need to change; that was the whole point of the corrective action. But she couldn't start there, because I would have become defensive, shut down and not taken responsibility. I still to this day think that my coworker should have been reprimanded. But I also own my part in it. I see that I went down that cowpath, and I know that I won't do it a second time.

The difference in the two feedback sessions illustrated above boils down to coaching, which deepens self-awareness and catalyzes growth, versus reprimanding, which sparks self-protection and avoidance of responsibility. To summarize, powerful, high-impact feedback conversations share the following elements:

1. An intention to help the employee grow, rather than to show him he was wrong. The feedback should increase, not drain, the employee's motivation and resources for change. When preparing for a feedback conversation as a manager, reflect

on what you hope to achieve and on what impact you'd like to have on the employee, perhaps by doing a short meditation just before the meeting.

2. Openness on the part of the feedback giver, which is essential to creating a high-quality connection that facilitates change. If you start off feeling uncomfortable and self-protective, your employee will match that energy, and you'll each leave the conversation frustrated with the other person.

3. Inviting the employee into the problem-solving process. You can ask questions such as: What ideas do you have? What are you taking away from this conversation? What steps will you take, by when, and how will I know?

Giving developmental feedback that sparks growth is a critical challenge to master, because it can make the difference between an employee who contributes powerfully and positively to the organization and one who feels diminished by the organization and contributes far less. A single conversation can switch an employee on—or shut her down. A true developmental leader sees the raw material for brilliance in every employee and creates the conditions to let it shine, even when the challenge is tough.

Monique Valcour is a management academic, coach, and consultant.

CHAPTER 13

Making Smart Decisions

A summary of the full-length HBR article "Why Good Leaders Make Bad Decisions" by **Andrew Campbell**, **Jo Whitehead**, *and* **Sydney Finkelstein**, *highlighting key ideas and company examples, and a checklist for putting the idea into action.*

IDEA IN BRIEF

- Leaders make decisions largely through unconscious processes that neuroscientists call pattern recognition and emotional tagging. These processes usually make for quick, effective decisions, but they can be distorted by bias.

Adapted from *Harvard Business Review*, February 2009 (product #R0902D)

- Managers need to find systematic ways to recognize the sources of bias—what the authors call "red flag conditions"—and then design safeguards that introduce more analysis, greater debate, or stronger governance. The authors identify three of these red flag conditions as the presence of:

  - Inappropriate self-interest, which, according to research, can bias even well-intentioned professionals such as doctors and auditors.

  - Distorting attachments to people, places, and things—for example, an executive's reluctance to sell a business unit they've worked in.

  - Misleading memories, which may seem relevant and comparable to the current situation but lead our thinking down the wrong path by obscuring important differentiating factors.

- By using the approach described in this article, companies will avoid many flawed decisions that are caused by the way our brains operate.

IDEA IN PRACTICE

Leaders make quick decisions by recognizing patterns in the situations they encounter, and then responding to the emotional associations attached to those patterns. Most of the time, the process works well, but it can result in serious mistakes when those emotional associations are biased.

Example: When Wang Laboratories launched its own personal computer, founder An Wang chose to create a proprietary operating system even though the IBM PC was clearly becoming the standard. This blunder was influenced by his belief that IBM had cheated him early in his career, which made him reluctant to consider using a system linked to an IBM product.

To guard against distorted decision making and strengthen the decision process, get the help of an independent person to identify which decision makers are likely to be affected by self-interest, emotional attachments, or misleading memories.

Example: The about-to-be-promoted head of the cosmetics business at one Indian company was considering whether to appoint her number-two as her successor. She recognized that her judgment might be distorted by her attachment to her colleague and by her vested interest in keeping her workload down during the transition. The executive asked a headhunter to evaluate her colleague and to determine whether better candidates could be found externally.

If the risk of distorted decision making is high, build safeguards into the decision process. Expose decision makers to additional experience and analysis, design in more debate and opportunities for challenge, add more oversight, and monitor whether the decision is generating the expected results.

Example: In helping the CEO make an important strategic decision, the chairman of one global

IDENTIFYING RED FLAGS

Red flags are useful only if they can be spotted before a decision is made. How can you recognize them in complex situations? We have developed the following seven-step process:

1. *Lay out the range of options.* It's never possible to list them all. But it's normally helpful to note the extremes. These provide boundaries for the decision.

2. *List the main decision makers.* Who is going to be influential in making the judgment calls and the final choice? There may be only one or two people involved. But there could also be 10 or more.

3. *Choose one decision maker to focus on.* It's usually best to start with the most influential person. Then identify red flag conditions that might distort that individual's thinking. Discuss with the individual if needed.

4. *Check for inappropriate self-interest or distorting attachments.* Is any option likely to be particularly attractive or unattractive to the decision maker because of personal interests or attachments to people, places, or things? Do any of these interests or attachments conflict with the objectives of the decision?

5. *Check for misleading memories.* What are the uncertainties in this decision? For each area of uncertainty, consider whether the decision maker might draw on potentially misleading memories. Think about past experiences that could mislead, especially ones with strong emotional associations. Think also about previous judgments that could now be unsound, given the current situation.

6. *Repeat the analysis with the next-most-influential person.* In a complex case, it may be necessary to consider many more people, and the process may bring to light a long list of possible red flags.

7. *Review the list of red flags you have identified for bias.* Determine whether the balance of red flags is likely to bias the decision in favor of or against some options. If so, put one or more safeguards in place. Biases can cancel each other out, so it is necessary to assess the balance taking account of the likely influence of each person involved in the decision.

chemical company encouraged the chief executive to seek advice from investment bankers, set up a project team to analyze options, and create a steering committee that included the chairman and the CFO to review the CEO's proposal.

Andrew Campbell is a director of the Ashridge Strategic Management Centre in England. **Jo Whitehead** (jo.whitehead@ashridge.org.uk) is a director of the Ashridge Strategic Management Centre in London. **Sydney Finkelstein** is the Steven Roth Professor of Management and Director of the Leadership Center at the Tuck School of Business at Dartmouth College. His new book is *Superbosses: How Exceptional Leaders Manage the Flow of Talent* (Portfolio/Penguin, 2016). Campbell, Whitehead, and Finkelstein are the coauthors of *Think Again: Why Good Leaders Make Bad Decisions and How to Keep It from Happening to You* (Harvard Business Review Press, 2008).

CHAPTER 14

An Emotional Strategy for Negotiations

by Alison Wood Brooks

It is, without questions, my favorite day of the semester—the day when I teach my MBA students a negotiation exercise called "Honoring the Contract."

I assign students to partners, and each reads a different account of a (fictitious) troubled relationship between a supplier (a manufacturer of computer components) and a client (a search engine startup). They learn that the two parties signed a detailed contract eight months earlier, but now they're at odds over several of

---

Reprinted from "Emotion and the Art of Negotiation" in *Harvard Business Review*, December 2015 (product #R1512C)

the terms (sales volume, pricing, product reliability, and energy efficiency specs). Each student assumes the role of either client or supplier and receives confidential information about company finances and politics. Then each pair is tasked with renegotiating—a process that could lead to an amended deal, termination of the contract, or expensive litigation.

What makes this simulation interesting, however, lies not in the details of the case but in the top-secret instructions given to one side of each pairing before the exercise begins: "Please start the negotiation with a display of anger. You must display anger for a minimum of 10 minutes at the beginning." The instructions go on to give specific tips for showing anger: Interrupt the other party. Call them "unfair" or "unreasonable." Blame them personally for the disagreement. Raise your voice.

Before the negotiations begin, I spread the pairs all over the building so that the students can't see how others are behaving. Then, as the pairs negotiate, I walk around and observe. Although some students struggle, many are spectacularly good at feigning anger. They wag a finger in their partner's face. They pace around. I've never seen the exercise result in a physical confrontation—but it has come close. Some of the negotiators who did not get the secret instructions react by trying to defuse the other person's anger. But some react angrily themselves—and it's amazing how quickly the emotional responses escalate. When I bring everyone back into the classroom after 30 minutes, there are always students still yelling at each other or shaking their heads in disbelief.

During the debriefing, we survey the pairs to see how angry they felt and how they fared in resolving the problem. Often, the more anger the parties showed, the more likely it was that the negotiation ended poorly—for example, in litigation or an impasse (no deal). Once I've clued the entire class in on the setup, discussion invariably makes its way to this key insight: Bringing anger to a negotiation is like throwing a bomb into the process, and it's apt to have a profound effect on the outcome.

Until 20 years ago, few researchers paid much attention to the role of emotions in negotiating—how feelings can influence the way people overcome conflict, reach agreement, and create value when dealing with another party. Instead, negotiation scholars focused primarily on strategy and tactics—particularly the ways in which parties can identify and consider alternatives, use leverage, and execute the choreography of offers and counteroffers. Scientific understanding of negotiation also tended to home in on the transactional nature of working out a deal: how to get the most money or profit from the process. Even when experts started looking at psychological influences on negotiations, they focused on diffuse and nonspecific moods—such as whether negotiators felt generally positive or negative, and how that affected their behavior.

Over the past decade, however, researchers have begun examining how specific emotions—anger, sadness, disappointment, anxiety, envy, excitement, and regret—can affect the behavior of negotiators. They've studied the differences between what happens when people simply feel these emotions and what happens when they also express them to the other party through words or actions. In negotiations that are less transactional and involve parties in long-term relationships, understanding the role of emotions is even more important than it is in transactional deal making.

This new branch of research is proving extremely useful. We all have the ability to regulate how we experience emotions, and specific strategies can help us improve tremendously in that regard. We also have some control over the extent to which we express our feelings—and again, there are specific ways to cloak (or emphasize) an expression of emotion when doing so may be advantageous. For instance, research shows that feeling or looking anxious results in suboptimal negotiation outcomes. So individuals who are prone to anxiety when brokering a deal can take certain steps both to limit their nervousness and to make it less obvious to their negotiation opponent. The same is true for other emotions.

In the pages that follow, I discuss—and share coping strategies for—many of the emotions people typically feel over the course of a negotiation. Anxiety is most likely to crop up before the process begins or during its early stages. We're prone to experience anger or excitement in the heat of the discussions. And we're most likely to feel disappointment, sadness, or regret in the aftermath.

Avoiding Anxiety

Anxiety is a state of distress in reaction to threatening stimuli—in particular, novel situations that have the potential for undesirable outcomes. In contrast to anger, which motivates people to escalate conflict (the "fight" part of the fight-or-flight response), anxiety trips the "flight" switch and makes people want to exit the scene.

Because patience and persistence are often desirable when negotiating, the urge to exit quickly is counterproductive. But the negative effects of feeling anxious while negotiating may go further. In my recent research, I wondered if anxious negotiators also develop low aspirations and expectations, which could lead them to make timid first offers—a behavior that directly predicts poor negotiating outcomes.

In work with Maurice Schweitzer in 2011, I explored how anxiety influences negotiations. First we surveyed 185 professionals about the emotions they expected to feel before negotiating with a stranger, negotiating to buy a car, and negotiating to increase their salary. When dealing with a stranger or asking for a higher salary, anxiety was the dominant emotional expectation; when negotiating for the car, anxiety was second only to excitement.

To understand how anxiety can affect negotiators, we then asked a separate group of 136 participants to negotiate a cell phone contract that required agreeing on a purchase price, a warranty period, and the length of the contract. We induced anxiety in half the participants by having them listen to continuous three-minute clips of the menacing theme music from the film *Psycho*, while the other half listened to pleasant music by Handel. (Researchers call this *incidental* emotional manipulation, and it's quite powerful. Listening to the *Psycho* music is genuinely uncomfortable: People's palms get sweaty, and some listeners become jumpy.)

In this experiment and three others, we found that anxiety had a significant effect on how people negotiated. People experiencing anxiety made weaker first offers, responded more quickly to each move the counterpart made, and were more likely to exit negotiations early (even though their instructions clearly warned that exiting early would reduce the value they received from the negotiation). Anxious negotiators made deals that were 12% less financially attractive than those made by negotiators in the neutral group. We did discover one caveat, however: People who gave themselves high ratings in a survey on negotiating aptitude were less affected by anxiety than others.

Those experiments examined what happens when people feel anxious. But what happens when they express that anxiety, making it clear to their counterparts that they're nervous (and perhaps vulnerable)? In 2012, with Francesca Gino and Maurice Schweitzer, I conducted eight experiments to explore how anxious people behaved in situations in which they could seek advice from others. We found that relative to people who did not feel anxious, they were less confident, more likely to consult others when making decisions, and less able to discriminate between good and bad advice. In the most relevant of these experiments, we found that anxious participants did not discount advice from someone with a stated conflict of interest, whereas subjects feeling neutral emotions looked upon that advice skeptically. Although this research didn't directly address how the subjects would negotiate, it suggests that people who express anxiety are more likely to be taken advantage of in a negotiation, especially if the other party senses their distress.

Excellent negotiators often make their counterparts feel anxious on purpose. For example, on the TV show *Shark Tank*, six wealthy investors ("sharks") negotiate with entrepreneurs hoping for funding. The entrepreneurs must pitch their ideas in front of a huge television audience and face questions from the investors that are often aggressive and unnerving. As this is going on, stress-inducing music fills the TV studio. This setup does more than create drama and entertainment for viewers; it also intentionally puts pressure on the entrepreneurs. The sharks are professional negotiators who want to knock the entrepreneurs off balance so that it will be easier to take ownership of their good ideas at the lowest price possible. (When multiple sharks want to invest, they often drop comments that are intended to make opposing investors anxious too.) If you watch the show closely, you'll probably notice a pattern: The entrepreneurs who seem least rattled by the environmental stressors tend to negotiate the most carefully and deliberately—and often strike the best deals.

The takeaway from both research and practice is clear: Try your utmost to avoid feeling anxious while negotiating. How can you manage that? Train, practice, rehearse, and keep sharpening your negotiating skills. Anxiety is often a response to novel stimuli, so the more familiar the stimuli, the more comfortable and the less anxious you will feel. (That's why clinicians who treat anxiety disorders often rely on exposure therapy: People who are nervous about flying on airplanes, for instance, are progressively exposed to the experience, first getting used to the sights and sounds, then sitting in airliner seats, and ultimately taking flights.) Indeed, although many people enroll in negotiation classes to learn strategies and increase skills, one of the primary benefits is the comfort that comes from repeatedly practicing deal making in simulations and exercises. Negotiation eventually feels more routine, so it's not such an anxiety-inducing experience.

Another useful strategy for reducing anxiety is to bring in an outside expert to handle the bargaining. Third-party negotiators will be less anxious because their skills are better honed, the process is routine for them, and they have a lower personal stake in the outcome. Outsourcing your negotiation may sound like a cop-out, but it's a frequent practice in many industries. Home buyers and sellers use real estate brokers partly for their negotiating experience; athletes, authors, actors, and even some business executives rely on agents to hammer out contracts. Although there are costs to this approach, they are often more than offset by the more favorable terms that can be achieved. And although anxious negotiators may have the most to gain from involving a third party (because anxiety can be a particularly difficult emotion to regulate in an uncomfortable setting), this strategy can also be useful when other negative emotions surface.

Managing Anger

Like anxiety, anger is a negative emotion, but instead of being self-focused, it's usually directed toward someone else. In most circumstances, we try to keep our tempers in check. When it comes to negotiating, however, many people believe that anger can be a productive emotion—one that will help them win a larger share of the pie.

This view stems from a tendency to view negotiations in competitive terms rather than collaborative ones. Researchers call this the *fixed-pie bias*: People, particularly those with limited experience making deals, assume that a negotiation is a zero-sum game in which their own interests conflict directly with a counterpart's. (More experienced negotiators, in contrast, look for ways to expand the pie through collaboration, rather than nakedly trying to snatch a bigger slice.) Anger, the thinking goes, makes one seem stronger, more powerful, and better able to succeed in this grab for value.

In fact, there's a body of research—much of it by Keith Allred, a former faculty member at Harvard's Kennedy School of Government—that documents the consequences of feeling angry while negotiating. This research shows that anger often harms the process by escalating conflict, biasing perceptions, and making impasses more likely. It also reduces joint gains, decreases cooperation, intensifies competitive behavior, and increases the rate at which offers are rejected. Angry negotiators are less accurate than neutral negotiators both in recalling their own interests and in judging other parties' interests. And angry negotiators may seek to harm or retaliate against their counterparts, even though a more cooperative approach might increase the value that both sides can claim from the negotiation.

Despite these findings, many people continue to see advantages to feeling or appearing angry. Some even attempt to turn up the volume on their anger, because they think it will make them more effective in a negotiation. In my own research, I have found that given a choice between feeling angry and feeling happy while negotiating, more than half the participants want to be in an angry state and view it as significantly advantageous.

There *are* cases when feeling angry can lead to better outcomes. Research by Gerben van Kleef at the University of Amsterdam demonstrates that in a one-time, transactional negotiation with few opportunities to collaborate to create value, an angry negotiator can wind up with a better deal. There may even be situations in which a negotiator decides to feign anger, because the counterpart, in an attempt to defuse that anger, is likely to give ground on terms. This might work well if you are haggling with a stranger to buy a car, for example.

But negotiators who play this card must be aware of the costs. Showing anger in a negotiation damages the long-term relationship between the parties. It reduces liking and trust. Research by Rachel Campagna at the University of New Hampshire shows that false representations of anger may generate small tactical benefits but also lead to considerable and persistent blowback. That is, faking anger can create authentic feelings of anger, which in turn diminish trust for both parties. Along the same lines, research by Jeremy Yip and Martin Schweinsberg demonstrates that people who encounter an angry negotiator are more likely to walk away, preferring to let the process end in a stalemate.

In many contexts, then, feeling or expressing anger as a negotiating tactic can backfire. So in most cases, tamping down any anger you feel—and limiting the anger you express—is a smarter strategy. This may be hard to do, but there are tactics that can help.

PREPARING YOUR EMOTIONAL STRATEGY

Preparation is key to success in negotiations. It's vital to give advance thought to the objective factors involved (Who are the parties? What are the issues? What is my best outside option if we don't reach a deal?), but it is perhaps even more important to prepare your emotional strategy. Use the following questions and tips to plan ahead for each stage of the negotiation.

	Ask yourself:	Remember:
The buildup	• How do I feel? • Should I express my emotions? • How might the people across the table feel? • Are they likely to hide or express their emotions? • Should I recruit a third party to negotiate on my behalf?	• It's normal to feel anxious and excited. • Try to avoid expressing anxiety. • Expressing forward-looking excitement may help build rapport. • In emotionally charged situations (such as a divorce), consider having a third party (such as a lawyer) negotiate on your behalf.
The main event	• What things could happen that would make me feel angry? • What things might I do that would trigger my counterparts to feel angry? • What might they do or ask that would make me feel anxious?	• Be careful about expressing anger; it may extract concessions but harm the long-term relationship. • Avoid angering your counterparts; they are likely to walk away. • Preparing answers to tough questions is critical for staying calm in the moment.
The finale	• What are the possible outcomes of the negotiation? What do I hope to achieve? What do I expect to achieve? • How would those outcomes make me feel? • Should I express those feelings? To whom? • How are my counterparts likely to feel about the possible outcomes?	• To reduce disappointment, outline clear aspirations and expectations and adjust them throughout the negotiation. • When you feel pleased about an outcome, it may be wise to keep it to yourself. • The best negotiators create value for everyone, claiming the lion's share for themselves but making their counterparts feel that they, too, won.

Building rapport before, during, and after a negotiation can reduce the odds that the other party will become angry. If you seek to frame the negotiation cooperatively—to make it clear that you're seeking a win-win solution instead of trying to get the lion's share of a fixed pie—you may limit the other party's perception that an angry grab for value will work well. If the other party does become angry, apologize. Seek to soothe. Even if you feel that his anger is unwarranted, recognize that you're almost certainly better positioned tactically if you can reduce the hostility.

Perhaps the most effective way to deal with anger in negotiations is to recognize that many negotiations don't unfold all at once but take place over multiple meetings. So if tensions are flaring, ask for a break, cool off, and regroup. This isn't easy when you're angry, because your fight-or-flight response urges you to escalate, not pull back. Resist that urge and give the anger time to dissipate. In heated negotiations, hitting the pause button can be the smartest play.

Finally, you might consider reframing anger as sadness. Though reframing one negative emotion as another sounds illogical, shared feelings of sadness can lead to cooperative concession making, whereas oppositional anger often leads to an impasse.

Handling Disappointment and Regret

It can be tempting to see negotiations in binary terms—you either win or lose. Of course, that is generally too simplistic: Most complex negotiations will end with each side having achieved some of its goals and not others—a mix of wins and losses. Still, as a negotiation winds down, it's natural to look at the nascent agreement and feel, on balance, more positive or negative about it.

Disappointment can be a powerful force when it's expressed to the other party near the end of the negotiation. There's a relationship between anger and disappointment—both typically arise when an individual feels wronged—and it's useful to understand how one can be used more constructively than the other. (Think back to how you reacted as a child if your parents said "I'm very disappointed in you" instead of "I'm very angry with you.") Although expressing anger may create defensiveness or increase the odds of a standoff, expressing disappointment can serve a more tactical purpose by encouraging the other party to look critically at her own actions and consider whether she wants to change her position to reduce the negative feelings she's caused you.

Research shows that one cause of disappointment in a negotiation is the speed of the process. When a negotiation unfolds or concludes too quickly, participants tend to feel dissatisfied. They wonder if they could or should have done more or pushed harder. Negotiation teachers see this in class exercises: Often the first students to finish up are the most disappointed by the outcome. The obvious way to lessen the likelihood of disappointment is to proceed slowly and deliberately.

Regret is slightly different from disappointment. While the latter tends to involve sadness about an outcome, someone feeling regret is looking a little more upstream, at the course of actions that led to this unhappy outcome, and thinking about the missteps or mistakes that created the disappointment.

Studies show that people are most likely to regret actions they didn't take—the missed opportunities and errors of omission, rather than errors of commission. That can be a powerful insight for negotiators, whose primary actions should be asking questions, listening, proposing solutions, and brainstorming new alternatives if the parties can't agree. Ironically, people often don't ask questions while negotiating: They may forget to raise important matters or feel reluctant to probe too deeply, deeming it invasive or rude. Those fears are often misplaced. In fact, people who ask a lot of questions tend to be better liked, and they learn more things.

In negotiations, information is king and learning should be a central goal. One way to reduce the potential for regret is to ask questions without hesitation. Aim to come away from the negotiation with the sense that every avenue was explored.

Skilled negotiators use another technique to minimize the odds of regret: the *post-settlement settlement*. This strategy recognizes that tension often dissipates when there's a deal on the table that makes everyone happy, and sometimes the best negotiating happens after that tension is released. So instead of shaking hands and ending the deal making, one party might say, "We're good. We have terms we can all live with. But now that we know we've reached an agreement, let's spend a few more minutes chatting to see if we can find anything that sweetens it for both sides." Done ineptly, this might seem as if one party is trying to renege or renegotiate. However, when handled deftly, a post-settlement settlement can open a pathway for both sides to become even more satisfied with the outcome and stave off regrets.

Tempering Happiness and Excitement

There isn't much research on how happiness and excitement affect negotiations, but intuition and experience suggest that expressing these emotions can have significant consequences. The National Football League prohibits and penalizes "excessive celebrations" after a touchdown or big play because such conduct can generate ill will. For the same reason, the "winner" in a deal should not gloat as the negotiations wrap up. Nonetheless, this happens all the time. In workshops, I routinely see students unabashedly boast and brag (sometimes to the entire class) about how they really stuck it to their opponents in a negotiation exercise. Not only do these students risk looking like jerks, but in a real-world setting, they might suffer more dire consequences: the other party might invoke a right of rescission, seek to renegotiate, or take punitive action the next time the parties need to strike a deal.

Although it's unpleasant to feel disappointed after a negotiation, it can be even worse to make your counterparts feel that way. And in certain situations, showing happiness or excitement triggers disappointment in others. The best negotiators achieve great deals for themselves but leave their opponents believing that they, too, did fabulously, even if the truth is different. In deals that involve a significant degree of future collaboration—say, when two companies agree to merge, or when an actor signs a contract with a producer to star in an upcoming movie—it can be appropriate to show excitement, but it's important to focus on the opportunities ahead rather than the favorable terms one party just gained.

Another danger of excitement is that it may increase your commitment to strategies or courses of action that you'd be better off abandoning. In my negotiation class, we do an exercise in which students must decide whether or not to send a race car driver into an important race with a faulty engine. Despite the risks, most students opt to go ahead with the race because they are excited and want to maximize their winnings. The exercise has parallels to a real-life example: the launch of the *Challenger* space shuttle. Though the engineers who designed the *Challenger*'s faulty O-ring had qualms about it, NASA managers were overly excited and determined to proceed with the launch. Their decision ultimately led to the craft's explosion and the loss of its seven crew members.

There are two lessons for negotiators here. First, be considerate: Do not let your excitement make your counterparts feel that they lost. Second, be skeptical: Do not let your excitement lead to overconfidence or an escalation of commitment with insufficient data.

Negotiating requires some of the same skills that playing poker does—a strategic focus, the imagination to see alternatives, and a knack for assessing odds, reading people, understanding others' positions, and bluffing when necessary. However, whereas the parties in a negotiation must strive for agreement, poker players make decisions unilaterally. Poker also lacks win-win outcomes or pie-sharing strategies: Any given hand is generally a zero-sum game, with one player's gains coming directly from the other players' pots.

MANAGING YOUR COUNTERPART'S EMOTIONS

Negotiating is an interpersonal process. There will always be at least one other party (and often many more) involved. In the adjoining article, I discuss how to manage your own emotions during a negotiation. But what about the other people at the table? Can you manage their emotions as well? I suggest two strategies for doing so:

1. *Be observant.* Perceiving how other people are feeling is a critical component of emotional intelligence, and it's particularly key in negotiations (as Adam Galinsky and his colleagues have found). So tune in to your counterpart's body language, tone of voice, and choice of words. When her verbal and nonverbal cues don't match up, ask questions. For example, "You are telling me you like this outcome, but you seem uneasy. Is something making you uncomfortable?" Or "You say you're angry, but you seem somewhat pleased. Are you truly upset about something? Or are you trying to intimidate me?"

(continued)

MANAGING YOUR COUNTERPART'S EMOTIONS

(*continued*)

Asking specific questions based on your perceptions of the other party's emotional expressions will make it easier for you to understand her perspective (a task people are shockingly bad at, according to research by Nicholas Epley). It will also make it difficult for a counterpart to lie to you; evidence suggests that people prefer to tell lies of omission about facts rather than lies of commission about feelings.

2. ***Don't be afraid to exert direct influence on your counterpart's emotions.*** This may sound manipulative or even unscrupulous, but you can use this influence for good. For example, if your counterpart seems anxious or angry, injecting humor or empathetic reassurance can dramatically change the tone of the interaction. By the same token, if your counterpart seems overconfident or pushy, expressing well-placed anger can inspire a healthy dose of fear.

In recent research with Elizabeth Baily Wolf, I have found that it's possible to go even further in managing others' emotions: You display an emotion, your counterpart sees it, and then you shape his interpretation of it. For example, imagine that you start crying at work. (Crying is a difficult-to-control and often embarrassing behavior.) Saying "I'm in tears because I'm passionate" rather than "I'm sorry I'm so emotional" can completely change the way others react and the way they view your self-control and competence.

Nonetheless, negotiators can learn a crucial lesson from the card table: the value of controlling the emotions we feel and especially those we reveal. In other words, good negotiators need to develop a poker face—not one that remains expressionless, always hiding true feelings, but one that displays the right emotions at the right times.

And although all human beings experience emotions, the frequency and intensity with which we do so differs from person to person. To be a better deal maker, conduct a thorough assessment of which emotions you are particularly prone to feel before, during, and after negotiations, and use techniques to minimize (or maximize) the experience and suppress (or emphasize) the expression of emotions as needed.

In one of my favorite scenes from the TV show *30 Rock*, hard-driving CEO Jack Donaghy (Alec Baldwin), who fancies himself an expert negotiator, explains to a colleague why he struck a poor deal: "I lost because of emotion, which I always thought was a weakness, but now I have learned can also be a weapon." Borrowing Jack's insightful metaphor, I urge you to wield your emotions thoughtfully. Think carefully about when to draw these weapons, when to shoot, and when to keep them safely tucked away in a hidden holster. Try to avoid feeling anxious, be careful about expressing anger, ask questions to circumvent disappointment and regret, and remember that happiness and excitement can have adverse consequences.

Just as you prepare your tactical and strategic moves before a negotiation, you should invest effort in preparing your emotional approach. It will be time well spent.

Alison Wood Brooks is an assistant professor at Harvard Business School. She teaches negotiation in the MBA and executive education curricula and is affiliated with the Behavioral Insights Group.

CHAPTER 15

Working Across Cultures

by Andy Molinsky

One of the greatest assets we have as natives of a culture is our ability to quickly "read" another person's emotions. Over time, we learn how to understand whether our colleagues are truly interested in a project or just giving it lip service by noticing the expression on their faces. We can tell when someone really likes something we've proposed by the way they react. And we can often detect motivation as well—whether someone is truly willing to put in the extra time and effort to make something happen—just by seeing the fire in their eyes or the passion in their voice.

Originally published on hbr.org on April 20, 2015, as "Emotional Intelligence Doesn't Translate Across Borders" (product #H020D6)

The problem, of course, comes when we cross cultures and venture into a completely different world of emotional expression. Emotions vary tremendously across cultures—both in terms of their expression and their meaning. Without a detailed understanding of these emotional landscapes, crossing cultures can become a communication minefield.

Take, for example, the expression of enthusiasm. In the United States, it's culturally acceptable, even admirable, to show enthusiasm in a business setting, assuming it's appropriate for the situation. When arguing for a point in a meeting, for example, it is quite appropriate to express your opinions passionately; it can help to convince those around you. Or when speaking with a potential employer at a networking event, it is often encouraged to express your interest quite enthusiastically; the employer may interpret how invested you are in a job based on your expressed eagerness.

In many other cultures, however, enthusiasm means something quite different. In Japan, for example, there are strict boundaries about when and where people are allowed to display emotion.[1] During the regular workday, Japanese individuals are not typically emotionally expressive. Even if they feel excited about their work, they will rarely show it explicitly. This often changes outside of the workplace setting, though, where Japanese people can show a great deal of emotion—for example, when drinking, having dinner with work colleagues, or singing karaoke. In China, self-control and modesty are the coin of the realm, not one's ability to outwardly express emotion.[2] In fact, expressing too much outward enthusiasm, especially in front of a boss, could be seen as showing off, which is not typically condoned in Chinese culture.

Given these differences and the importance of getting it right when communicating across cultures, what are thoughtful managers to do?

A first tip is to treat emotions like another language. If you're traveling or moving to France, you're bound to learn French, or at least some key phrases. Treat emotions in the same way. Try your best to learn the language of emotions in whatever culture you're working in. Observe whether people tend to express emotions readily or keep them to themselves, and if, as in the Japan example above, there are differences in when and where people freely express emotion. Diagnose any gaps between how you'd express emotions in your culture and how people you'll be interacting with express emotion in theirs.

In addition to learning the language of emotions, make sure you also learn how to respond constructively when you do encounter emotions different from your own. For example, if you're expecting a smile from your boss after suggesting a new idea but instead get a blank stare, don't necessarily assume she hates you or your idea. Instead, gather more information to fully understand her point of view. You might ask a follow-up question to get a better sense of her opinion: Ask if your proposal was clear or if she felt your idea addressed the concerns she had. Keep in mind that cultural norms differ in terms of how appropriate it might be to ask questions like these to your boss, but the general idea is to do what you can to collect data to help you decipher emotional expressions, rather than relying solely on your initial, knee-jerk reaction or presumption.

———————

Andy Molinsky is a professor of international management and organizational behavior at the Brandeis International Business School. He is the author of *Global Dexterity* (Harvard Business Review Press, 2013) and the new book *Reach: A New Strategy to Help You Step Outside Your Comfort Zone, Rise to the Challenge, and Build Confidence* (Penguin Random House, 2017). Follow Andy on Twitter @andymolinsky.

NOTES

1. Fumiyo Araki and Richard L. Wiseman, Emotional Expressions in the United States and Japan," *International Communication Studies* 6, no. 2 (1996).

2. Ibid.

Dealing with Difficult People

CHAPTER 16

Make Your Enemies Your Allies

by Brian Uzzi and Shannon Dunlap

John Clendenin was fresh out of business school in 1984 when he took on his first managerial position, in Xerox's parts and supply division. He was an obvious outsider: young, African American, and a former Marine, whose pink shirts and brown suits stood out amid the traditional gray and black attire of his new colleagues. "I was strikingly different," he recalls. And yet his new role required him to lead a team including employees who had been with Xerox for decades.

Reprinted from *Harvard Business Review*, May 2012 (product #R1205K)

One of his direct reports was Tom Gunning, a 20-year company veteran who believed Clendenin's job should have gone to him, not to a younger, nontechnical newcomer. Gunning also had a cadre of pals on the team. As a result, Clendenin's first days were filled with strained smiles and behind-the-back murmurs. Though he wasn't looking for adversaries, "I knew these guys were discontented about me coming in," Clendenin remembers.

He was right to be wary. Anyone who has faced a rival at work—a colleague threatened by your skills, a superior unwilling to acknowledge your good ideas, or a subordinate who undermines you—knows such dynamics can prove catastrophic for your career, and for your group or organization. When those with formal or informal power are fighting you, you may find it impossible to accomplish—or get credit for—any meaningful work.

And even if you have the upper hand, an antagonistic relationship inevitably casts a cloud over you and your team, sapping energy, stymieing progress, and distracting group members from their goals.

Because rivalries can be so destructive, it's not enough to simply ignore, sidestep, or attempt to contain them. Instead, effective leaders turn rivals into collaborators—strengthening their positions, their networks, and their careers in the process. Think of these relationships not as chronic illnesses you have to endure but as wounds that must be treated in order for you to lead a healthy work life.

Here we share a method, called the 3Rs (using *redirection, reciprocity,* and *rationality*), for efficiently and effectively turning your adversaries into your allies. If you execute each step correctly, you will develop new "connective tissue" within your organization, boosting your ability to broker knowledge and drive fresh thinking. The method is drawn from our own inductive case studies—including interviews with business leaders such as John Clendenin, who agreed to let us tell his story in this article—and from empirical research conducted by Brian and others investigating the physiology of the brain, the sociology of relationships, and the psychology of influence.

Emotions and Trust

Many well-intentioned efforts to reverse rivalries fail in large part because of the complex way trust operates in these relationships. Research shows that trust is based on both reason and emotion. If the emotional orientation toward a person is negative—typically because of a perceived threat—then reason will be twisted to align with those negative feelings. This is why feuds can stalemate trust: New facts and arguments, no matter how credible and logical, may be seen as ploys to dupe the other side. This effect is not just psychological; it is physiological. When we experience negative emotions, blood recedes from the thinking part of the brain, the cerebral cortex, and rushes to its oldest and most involuntary part, the "reptilian" stem, crippling the intake of new information.

Most executives who decide they want to reverse a rivalry will, quite understandably, turn to reason, presenting incentives for trustworthy collaboration. But in these situations, the "emotional brain" must be managed before adversaries can understand evidence and be persuaded.

When John Clendenin looked at Tom Gunning at Xerox, he immediately saw grounds for a strong partnership beyond a perfunctory subordinate-superior relationship. Gunning had 20 years' worth of organizational and technical knowledge, and contacts around the company, but he lacked the leadership skills and vision that Clendenin possessed. Conversely, Clendenin understood management but needed Gunning's expertise and connections to successfully navigate his new company. Unfortunately, Gunning's emotions were getting in the way. Clendenin needed to employ the 3Rs.

Redirection

Step 1 is to redirect your rival's negative emotions so that they are channeled away from you. Clendenin decided to have a one-on-one meeting with Gunning, but not in his office, because that would only remind Gunning of the promotion he'd lost. Instead, he found out where Gunning liked to eat and took him there for lunch. "I was letting him know that I understood his worth," Clendenin says of this contextual redirection.

He followed this with a plain statement of redirection, telling Gunning that a third entity beyond the control of both men was the root cause of their situation. "I didn't put you in this position," Clendenin said. "Xerox put us both in this position."

Many executives scoff when they first hear this story, believing Clendenin's actions to be too transparent. But redirection doesn't have to be hidden. With stage magic, for example, audience members understand that redirection is happening, but that doesn't lessen their acceptance or spoil the payoff of the technique. Other personal interactions work similarly. For instance, we accept flattery even if we recognize it as such.

Another common redirection tactic is to introduce a discussion of things you and your rival have in common, or casually portray a source of tension—a particular initiative, employee, or event—in a more favorable light. It sounds obvious. But redirection will shift negative emotions away from you and lay the groundwork for Step 2: reciprocity.

Reciprocity

The essential principle here is to *give before you ask*. Undoing a negative tie begins with giving up something of value rather than asking for a "fair trade." If you give and then ask for something right away in return, you don't establish a relationship; you carry out a transaction.

When done correctly, reciprocity is like priming the pump. In the old days, pumps required lots of exertion to produce any water. You had to repeatedly work a lever to eliminate a vacuum in the line before water could flow. But if you poured a small bucket of water into the line first, the vacuum was quickly eliminated, enabling the water to flow with less effort. Reciprocity with a rival works in much the same way.

Reflect carefully on *what* you should give. Ideally, choose something that requires little effort from the other party to reciprocate. Clendenin moved from redirection to reciprocity at the lunch by promising to support Gunning's leadership development and future advancement at Xerox. But, recognizing that mere promises of future returns wouldn't be enough to spark collaboration, he also offered Gunning something concrete: the chance to attend executive-level meetings. This was of immediate value, not a distant, murky benefit. Gunning could gain visibility, credibility, and connections.

The arrangement also ensured reciprocity. Gunning's presence at the meetings furnished Clendenin with on-hand technical expertise and organizational knowledge while giving him "reputation points" with Gunning's contacts. Thus, Clendenin's offer created the purest form of reciprocity; if Gunning attended the meetings, Clendenin would never have to explicitly request a quid pro quo.

Reciprocity involves considering ways that you can immediately fulfill a rival's need or reduce a pain point. Live up to your end of the bargain first, but figure out a way to ensure a return from your rival without the person's feeling that pressure. Another example comes from Brian's colleague Adam Galinsky, who advises leaders in contentious restructurings and business closings to generate goodwill among outgoing employees by offering professional references or placements at other companies as long as the employees continue to meet or exceed expectations until their office closes. The employees see immediate value, and although they don't consciously pay back the organization, the firm nonetheless benefits by maintaining continuity in its workforce until the scheduled closure.

Similarly, a colleague who helps an adversary complete a project or a subordinate who stays overtime to finish a task for a difficult boss not only help themselves but can reap rewards when other teammates or superiors benefit from that effort, too. Here the judicious giving before asking sets a foundation for reciprocity with third parties, whose buy-in can positively assist in reshaping the adversarial relationship. (See the sidebar "Rivalries Don't Exist in a Vacuum.")

Rationality

Step 3, rationality, establishes the expectations of the fledgling relationship you've built using the previous steps so that your efforts don't come off as dishonest or as ineffective pandering. What would have happened if Clendenin had left the lunch without explaining how he wanted to work with Gunning going forward? Gunning might have begun to second-guess his new boss's intentions and resumed his adversarial stance. If a rival is worried about the other shoe dropping, his emotional unease can undermine the trust you've built.

To employ rationality, Clendenin told Gunning that he needed him, or someone like him, to reach his goals at Xerox. This made it clear that he saw Gunning as a valuable, but not indispensable, partner. Another, softer approach might have involved Clendenin's giving Gunning "the right of first refusal" to collaborate with him, making the offer seem special while judiciously indicating that there were others who could step in. Just to be clear, Clendenin was not asking Gunning for a specific favor in exchange for the one he'd granted in Step 2. He was simply saying that he wanted him to become an ally.

Clendenin also reinforced the connection between the three steps by making his offer time-limited, which raised the perception of the value of the deal without changing its content. He told Gunning he needed an answer before they left the restaurant. "I needed to nip this in the bud," Clendenin recalls. "He knew I didn't care if we sat in that restaurant until midnight if we had to."

When rationality follows redirection and reciprocity, it should push your adversary into considering the situ-

RIVALRIES DON'T EXIST IN A VACUUM

Even when a leader executes the 3Rs flawlessly to end a rivalry, his work isn't necessarily done. That's because the relationship is often about more than just the two individuals. We all know people who seek to play to their advantage antagonism between others; some third parties might even view a blossoming partnership with trepidation or envy, triggering new negative emotions and rivalries.

You can head off this problem, as John Clendenin did, by framing your work as beneficial not just to you and your adversary but to the whole organization, which makes the reversal of rivalry in everyone's interest. When Clendenin brought Tom Gunning into those executive-level meetings, he made it clear that Gunning was going to be a "poster child" for a new age at Xerox, in which talented, long-term employees could find new paths to leadership in a time of corporate transition. Even if the conflictmongers didn't care about Clendenin's and Gunning's success, it would be far more difficult for them to sabotage an effort that was obviously good for the company.

ation from a reasoned standpoint, fully comprehending the expectations and benefits, and recognizing that he is looking at a valued opportunity that could be lost. Most people are highly motivated to avoid a loss, which complements their desire to gain something. Rationality is like offering medicine after a spoonful of sugar: It ensures that you're getting the benefit of the shifted negative emotions, and any growing positive ones, which would otherwise diffuse over time. And it avoids the ambiguity that clouds expectations and feedback when flattery and favors come one day, and demands the next.

Of course, Clendenin and Gunning did not walk out of the restaurant as full-blown collaborators. But both accepted that they should give each other the benefit of the doubt. Over the following weeks, this new mindset allowed them to work as allies, a process that deepened trust and resource-sharing in a self-reinforcing cycle. In this way, a potentially debilitating rivalry was transformed into a healthy working relationship and, in time, a strong partnership. Several years later, when Clendenin moved to another Xerox unit, he nominated Gunning as his replacement—and Gunning excelled in the position. The foundation for that remarkable shift had been established during the span of a single lunch.

Adapting the 3Rs

A key advantage of the 3Rs is that the method can work to reverse all kinds of rivalries, including those with a peer or a superior. Later in Clendenin's tenure at Xerox, he noticed an inefficiency in the company's inventory systems. At the time, Xerox was made up of semiautonomous international units that stockpiled excess inventory to avoid shortages. Clendenin proposed that the units instead share their inventories through an intrafirm network that would improve resource use and lower carrying costs for the company as a whole. Although the idea was objectively good for Xerox, it threatened the power of some unit vice presidents, so when Clendenin floated his idea, they shot it down.

WHAT IF THE 3RS FAIL?

The 3Rs are effective, but they aren't a guarantee of defusing resistance. What should you do if the strategy isn't working?

Strive for collaboration indirectly. For example, work well with a third party whom your rival trusts. A common ally can highlight to him the benefits of working with you.

Remember that timing matters. People in power need a reason to interact. This was certainly the case with John Clendenin's inventory-management pitch to the Xerox VPs: At first rebuffed, he was able to refloat his idea when the CEO called for a new strategy.

Recognize when to look elsewhere. Sometimes the effort needed to reverse a rivalry is so great, and the returns so low, for you and your company that you're better off deploying the same resources in another relationship.

A short time later, however, following an unexpected announcement by the CEO that the company needed better asset management, Clendenin found a way to re-introduce his proposal to the VPs. Because he knew they viewed him as an unwelcome challenger—or rival—he used the 3Rs.

His first move was to redirect their negative emotions away from him by planning a lunch for them at the regional office and serving them himself. This showed deference. He also presented himself not as an individual pushing a proposal but as someone who could expedite organizational change, shifting the reference point of his rivals' tension. "With all of those egos and personalities, I never said, 'This is my idea,'" Clendenin recalls. "I always said 'we.'"

Applying the reciprocity principle of "give before you ask," he requested nothing from them at the meeting. Instead, he facilitated a discussion about the CEO-led initiative. Inventory management was, unsurprisingly, a problem cited by many of the VPs, and Clendenin's facilitation brought that to light. He then took on the luster of the person who had illuminated a generic problem, rather than someone who wanted to lessen the VPs' autonomy.

That allowed him to present the rationality of his original idea. All of a sudden, it looked like an opportunity—rather than a threat—to the formerly antagonistic group. Clendenin indicated that he would be willing to coordinate a new system more cheaply than anyone else in the market could offer, while also noting that he might not have time to do so in the future, which raised the perceived value of his offer. The VPs agreed to execute the plan in stages and put Clendenin in charge. The initiative grew in small but steady steps, eventually saving Xerox millions. Equally important, Clendenin's embrace by his rivals positioned him as a broker in the company and burnished his reputation as an institution builder.

John Clendenin understood that rivalries help no one; indeed, success often depends on not just neutralizing your foes but turning them into collaborators. By using the 3Rs to build trust, Clendenin made sure everyone in his network thrived—including himself, Gunning, their team, the VPs, and Xerox—forming the basis for long-term ties and shared success. Years later, Clendenin started his own international logistics company. His partner in this new endeavor was his old rival, Tom Gunning, and the lead investors were none other than the unit VPs from Xerox who had once shot down his ideas.

Brian Uzzi is the Richard L. Thomas Professor of Leadership and Organizational Change at Northwestern's Kellogg School of Management and the codirector of the Northwestern Institute on Complex Systems (NICO). Shannon Dunlap is a journalist and writer based in New York City.

CHAPTER 17

How to Deal with a Passive-Aggressive Colleague

by Amy Gallo

Your colleague says one thing in a meeting but then does another. He passes you in the hallway without saying hello and talks over you in meetings. But when you ask to speak with him about it, he insists that everything's fine and the problem is all in your head. Argh! It's so frustrating to work with someone who is acting passive-

---

Adapted from content posted on hbr.org on January 11, 2016 (product #H02LQP) aggressively. Do you address the behavior directly? Or try to ignore it? How can you get to the core issue when your colleague pretends that nothing's going on?

What the Experts Say

It's not uncommon for colleagues to occasionally make passive-aggressive remarks to one another over particularly sensitive issues or when they feel they can't be direct. "We're all guilty of doing it once in a while," says Amy Su, coauthor of *Own the Room: Discover Your Signature Voice to Master Your Leadership Presence.* But persistent passive-aggressive behavior is a different ball game. "These are people who will often do anything to get what they need, including lie," says Annie McKee, founder of the Teleos Leadership Institute and coauthor of *Primal Leadership: Unleashing the Power of Emotional Intelligence.* In these cases, you have to take special precautions that help you and, hopefully, your counterpart both get your jobs done. Here are some tips:

Don't Get Caught Up

When your coworker pretends nothing is going on or accuses you of overreacting, it's hard not to get angry and defensive. But, McKee says, "This is not one of those situations to fight fire with fire." Do your best to remain calm. "The person may want you to get mad so they can then blame you, which is a release of their own anxiety," Su explains. "Responding in an emotional way will likely leave you looking—and feeling—like the fool. This is your opportunity to be the bigger person."

Consider What's Motivating the Behavior

People who routinely act in a passive-aggressive way aren't necessarily complete jerks. It could be that they don't know how to communicate or are afraid of conflict. McKee says that passive-aggressive behavior is often a way for people to "get their emotional point across without having true, healthy conflict." There's also a self-centeredness to it. "They make the flawed assumption that others should know what they're feeling and that their needs and preferences are more important than others'," says Su. Understand this, but don't try to diagnose all your colleague's problems. "You just have to see it for what it is," Su adds, "an unproductive expression of emotions that they can't share constructively."

Own Your Part

Chances are that you're not blameless in the situation. Ask yourself if something you're doing is contributing to the dynamic or causing the person to be passive-aggressive. "Own your half," says Su. Also, consider whether you've dished out the same behavior. "It can happen to even the best of us, whether we're procrastinating or wanting to avoid something. We might leak emotions in a way that's hurtful to others," says Su.

Focus on the Content, Not the Delivery

It might be the last thing you want to do, but try to see the situation from your colleague's perspective. What is the underlying opinion or perspective she's attempting to convey with her snarky comment? "Analyze the position the person is trying to share with you," says McKee. Does she think that the way you're running the project isn't working? Or does she disagree about your team goals? "Not everyone likes or knows how to publicly discuss or express what they think," says Su. If you can focus on the underlying business concern or question rather than the way she's expressing herself, you can move on to addressing the actual problem.

Acknowledge the Underlying Issue

Once you're calm and able to engage in a productive conversation, go back to the person. Say something like: "You made a good point in that exchange we had the other day. Here's what I heard you saying." This will help them talk about the substance of their concerns. "By joining *with* them, you have a better chance of turning the energy around," McKee explains. Do this in a matter-of-fact way, without discussing how the sentiment was expressed. "Don't listen or give any credence to the toxic part," advises Su. "Sometimes it's that they just want their opinion heard."

Watch Your Language

Whatever you say, don't accuse the person of being passive-aggressive. "That can hurt your cause," says McKee. Su agrees: "It's such a loaded word. It would put someone who's already on the defensive into a more angry position. Don't label or judge them." Instead, McKee suggests recounting how some of your previous interactions have played out and explaining the impact it's having on you and possibly others. If feasible, show that the behavior is working against something your counterpart cares about, like achieving the team's goals.

Find Safety in Numbers

You don't have to deal with this situation alone. "It's OK to reality-check with others and have allies in place to say you're not crazy," says Su. But be sure to frame your discussions as an attempt to constructively improve the relationship, so it doesn't come across as gossiping or bad-mouthing your colleague. Su suggests you ask something like: "I was wondering how Susan's comment landed with you. How did you interpret that?"

Set Guidelines for Everyone

You might also enlist the help of others in coming up with a long-term solution. "As a team, you can build healthy norms," McKee says. Together, you can agree to be more up-front about frustrations and model the honest and direct interactions you want to happen. You can also keep one another accountable. If your problematic colleague tends to ignore agreements, you might take notes in meetings about who's supposed to do what by when, so there are clear action items. The worst offenders are likely to give in to the positive peer pressure and public accountability.

Get Help in Extreme Situations

When a colleague persistently tries to undermine you or prevent you from doing your job, and outside observers confirm your take on the situation, you might have to go further. "If you share the same manager, you may be able to ask for help," says McKee. You might tell your boss: "A lot of us have noticed a particular behavior, and I want to talk about how it's impacting my ability to do my work." But she warns, "Step into those waters carefully. Your manager may be hoodwinked by the person and may not see the same behaviors, or be conflict-averse himself and not want to see it."

Protect Yourself

"If there's an interdependence in your work, make sure you're meeting your commitments and deadlines," Su says. "Copy others on important emails. Don't let that person speak for you or represent you in meetings. After a meeting, document agreements and next steps." McKee also suggests keeping records: "Track specific behaviors so that you have examples if needed. It's hard to argue with the facts." She also recommends you try to avoid working with the person and "keep contact to a minimum. If you have to work together, do it in a group setting" where your colleague is likely to be on better behavior. You might not be able to break their passive-aggressive habits, but you can control your reaction to any incidents.

Principles to Remember

Do:

- Understand why people typically act this way—
  their needs probably aren't being met

- Focus on the message your colleague is trying to convey, even if their delivery is misguided

- Take a step back and ask yourself if you're contributing to the issue in some way

Don't:

- Lose your cool—address the underlying business issue in a calm, matter-of-fact way

- Accuse the person of acting passive-aggressively—that will only make them madder

- Assume you can change your colleague's behavior

Case Study #1: Make Your Coworker Publicly Accountable

One of Neda Khosla's coworkers (names and details have been changed) in the student guidance office of the public high school where she worked was making things difficult for her. "He would agree to a plan in a meeting but then sabotage it by not following through," she explains. Her colleague, Gareth, defended himself by saying things like "That's not how I remember it" or "I didn't think we had finalized the plan." She tried to talk about these "misunderstandings" with him, but he always shrugged her off: "He'd say he was busy or didn't have time to talk," she recounted.

When Neda told Jim, her and Gareth's boss, that a certain project hadn't gotten done because of this strange dynamic, Jim said that he had noticed the pattern too. Together, they devised a plan to make Gareth more accountable. "He and I agreed that he would publicly ask for a volunteer to take notes on each meeting, [documenting] who would be responsible for accomplishing each task and by when," Neda recalls. She was the first volunteer.

And the approach worked. After Neda sent around the task list, Gareth couldn't make excuses. He was accountable to everyone who attended the meetings. And Neda didn't mind the additional work: "The extra effort I put in was less than the time I was spending fuming about my coworker and running around to pick up the pieces of the things he didn't complete. It actually helped everyone in our department be more productive and was something we should have done a long time ago."

Case Study #2: Get Help Sooner Rather Than Later

James Armstrong, a digital marketing consultant for Roman Blinds Direct, used to manage an eight-person team at a digital marketing agency. He had gotten the promotion three months after one of his direct reports, Violet, joined the agency, and she clearly wasn't thrilled to suddenly have him as a new boss. But "she was a top performer and extremely competent," James recalls, and since they'd worked "fairly harmoniously together as colleagues," he was happy to have her in the group.

Unfortunately, Violet became very difficult to manage. She didn't communicate with him unless absolutely necessary; she didn't actively engage in training sessions that he offered; and she "poked holes" in his initiatives. "She took every opportunity to make it clear that she didn't value my input," he explains.

Surprised and dismayed by her attitude, he decided to address it as he would with any other team member: "directly and clearly." He started by asking her in their one-on-one meetings whether something was wrong. She said there wasn't, but the behavior persisted, so he tried taking her out to coffee and asking whether he had unknowingly offended her or if she wanted to be managed in a different way. She acknowledged that there was a "personality clash," but she ended the conversation there and continued to treat him dismissively at the office. He heard from other staff members that she had even called him "lazy and useless."

"The last thing I wanted was to pass the issue further up the chain and potentially harm Violet's career," he says. After all, she was a valuable team member and he wanted to protect her. But, he reflects, "I should have immediately approached my manager." When he eventually did, she pointed out that his failure to effectively manage a key team member amounted to poor performance on his part.

Within a year, both James and Violet voluntarily left the agency, but neither was happy with the circumstances. He says that if he could do it over again, he would have talked to his manager sooner, kept better records on Violet's "toxic attitude," and when there weren't drastic improvements, fired her "without hesitation."

———————

Amy Gallo is a contributing editor at *Harvard Business Review* and the author of the *HBR Guide to Dealing with Conflict*. She writes and speaks about workplace dynamics. Follow her on Twitter @amyegallo.

CHAPTER 18

What to Do If You're a Toxic Handler

by Sandra L. Robinson and Kira Schabram

Divani (not her real name) is a senior analyst at a large telecommunications firm. She proudly describes herself as her department's "resident cheer-upper." As she says, "I have always been the person that people turn to for support . . . I listen really well and I like to listen, I like to help." But the year before I spoke to her, Divani's organization was going through a major change initiative: "I already had so much on my plate, and so many colleagues were leaning on me—turning to me to process,

---

Adapted from "When You're the Person Your Colleagues Always Vent To" posted on hbr.org on January 11, 2016 (product #H03A8W)

commiserate, ask for advice. It was hard to get through my own deadlines and also be there for my coworkers. I was drowning in stress and nearing burnout." She told us about feeling down on Sunday nights, feeling increasingly angry and cynical, and having trouble sleeping because she couldn't "shut my mind off." She took up smoking again after having given it up for four years and let her exercise routine falter.

Divani is what former Sauder School of Business professor Peter Frost and one of us (Sandra) have termed a *toxic handler*, someone who voluntarily shoulders the sadness, frustration, bitterness, and anger that are endemic to organizational life just as joy and success are. Toxic handlers can be found at all levels of the organization, particularly in roles that span disparate groups. And they are by no means confined to management roles. Their work is difficult and critical even if it often goes uncelebrated; it keeps organizations positive and productive even as the individuals within them necessarily clash and tussle. By carrying others' confidences, suggesting solutions to interpersonal issues, working behind the scenes to prevent pain, and reframing difficult messages in constructive ways, toxic handlers absorb the negativity in day-to-day professional life and allow employees to focus on constructive work.

This isn't easy work. And as Sandra's and Peter Frost's research of over 70 toxic handlers (or those who managed them) revealed, individuals in these roles frequently experience untenably high levels of stress and strain, which affect their physical health and career paths and often mean they have a diminished capacity to help others in the long run—a side effect that is most troubling for handlers.

But if handlers can recognize that they're playing a role that is both highly valuable *and* burdensome, they can see their own emotional competence in a new light and recognize the signs of serious strain while there's still something they can do about it.

How do you know if *you're* a toxic handler? Here are some questions to ask yourself:

- Are you working in an organizational character-ized by lots of change, dysfunction, or politics?

- Are you working in a role that spans different groups or different levels?

- Do you spend a lot of time listening to and offering advice to colleagues at work?

- Do people come to you to unload their worries, emotions, secrets, or workplace problems?

- Do you have a hard time saying "no" to colleagues, especially when they need you?

- Do you spend time behind the scenes, managing politics and influencing decisions so others are protected?

- Do you tend to mediate communication between a toxic individual and others?

- Are you that person who feels compelled to stand up for the people at work that need your help?

- Do you think of yourself as a counselor, mediator, or peacemaker?

If you've answered "yes" to four or more of these questions, then you may be a toxic handler. Before you panic at that label, recognize that there are both positives and negatives to fulfilling this role. On the positive side, being a toxic handler means you have valuable emotional strengths: You're probably a good listener; you're empathetic; you're good at suggesting solutions instead of piling on problems. The people around you value the support you provide. It's important, too, to understand that this role is strategically critical to organizations: You likely defuse tough situations and reduce dysfunction.

Now for the bad news. Chances are that you're taking on more work than is covered in your formal job description (and in fact, as an unsung hero, you may not be getting any kind of formal credit from the organization for these efforts and how much you bring to them). Listening, mediating, and working behind the scenes to protect others takes important time away from your other responsibilities. More importantly, it also takes tremendous emotional energy to listen, comfort, and counsel. As you are not a trained therapist, you may also be inadvertently taking on others' pain and slowly paying a price for it. Sandra's research shows that toxic handlers tend to take on others' emotions but have no way to offload them. Quite likely, as a person who is constantly helping others, you may be unlikely to be seeking support for yourself. And lastly, this role may be part of your identity, something that brings you fulfillment and in which you take satisfaction—and so it is difficult to step away from.

Consider Sheung-Li (not his real name). His manager was a star with a great track record, but he created a lot of turmoil. He wouldn't take the time to get to know anyone on Sheung-Li's team personally and totally disregarded more junior members. He was also obsessed with lofty performance goals that seemed to come out of nowhere. "My main role became protecting my team, reassuring them, keeping them focused on our objectives and away from the tensions this guy continually created," Sheung-Li described. "I spent an inordinate amount of time massaging the message, trying to convince my boss to reconsider his decisions so as to avoid the obvious fallout they would bring, playing mediator when our team was not delivering. I felt like I was treading water all the time. And I'm not even sure I was protecting my team from the pain he was causing. I was losing sleep over what was happening to my team, I had lost weight, and I was starting to get sick with one bug after another. I don't know if that was the cause but I know this was a really tough time in my life. It was hard to concentrate on anything else."

So if Sheung-Li's and Divani's stories sound familiar, how can you continue to help to your colleagues (and your organization!) while also protecting yourself? How can you keep playing your valuable role in a *sustainable* way?

Start by assessing whether the role is indeed taking a toll. Some toxic handlers are able to naturally take on more than others; you need to know what's right for you at any given time. Look for evidence of strain and burnout: physical symptoms like insomnia, jaw pain and TMJ, heart palpitations, more sickness than usual. Do you have a shorter fuse than you used to, or an inability to concentrate? Sometimes these symptoms can sneak up on you, so it may help to check in with others to see if they've noticed a change. If you're not experiencing stress as a result, there's nothing you need to change other than being aware and keeping an eye out. Being a toxic handler only needs to be "fixed" if it's actually hurting you. Here's how:

Reduce symptoms of stress

Turn to tried-and-true methods for stress relief: meditation, exercise, enough sleep, and healthful eating. Because toxic handlers have trouble doing things just for themselves, keep in mind that you're helping your colleagues by taking care of yourself. Set your colleagues as your intention for your meditation or yoga practice.

Pick your battles

It's hard to ask yourself where you'll have the most impact if you're emotionally drawn to every problem, but it's an exercise that will allow you to be more helpful where you can actually make a difference. Who is likely to be fine without your help? In which situations have you not even made a dent, despite your best efforts? Step away from these interactions.

Learn to say "no"

It's hard to say no to things you want to do, but it's important. Here's how to do it while still being supportive:

- Convey empathy. Make it clear that you feel for your colleague in their pain—you're not denying that they are having a legitimate emotional response to a situation.

- Tell them you're currently not in a position to be most helpful to them right now and, to the extent you are comfortable, explain the reasons why.

- Consider alternative sources of support. Refer your colleague to another person in the organization, or someone having a similar experience (so they can provide mutual support to one another). Suggest an article, book, or other resource on the topic (e.g., something on managing conflict or handling office politics). Or, if you know from experience that the person is good at coming up with creative solutions themselves, you can simply offer them encouragement to do so.

Let go of the guilt

If you feel guilty that you're not stepping in to help someone, here are some things to consider:

- Recognize that conflicts are often better solved by the parties directly involved. If you're stepping in repeatedly, you're not helping people acquire the skills and tools they need to succeed.

- Question whether you are truly the only one that can help in a particular situation. Enlist trusted others in the organization to help you think through this—you may identify a way to share the load.

- Remember that there is only so much of you to go around: Saying yes to one more person necessarily means that you are agreeing to do less for those people and projects you have already committed to.

Form a community

Find other toxic handlers to turn to for support—these could be others in similar roles in your organization, or other team members whom you see dealing with the fallout from the same toxic leader. You can also identify a pal to vent to or create a more formal group that comes together regularly to share their experiences. This is a particularly good option if your whole team or organization is going through turmoil and you know there are others experiencing the same challenges. Keep these outlets from turning into repetitive venting sessions by focusing the conversation on creative problem solving and advice.

Take breaks

These can be as small or as dramatic as you need. Divani started working with her door closed, which she had never done before. "I felt terrible about this, as if I was abandoning my coworkers who needed me. But if I lost my job, I wasn't going to be much good to anybody," she explained. Consider giving yourself a mental health day off of work or planning a significant vacation. In more dramatic situations, you could also consider a temporary reassignment of your role; because jobs that require you to mediate between multiple teams or groups tend to come under particular fire, you're more likely to get the respite you need if you are able to step away from that role for a time.

These breaks don't need to be forever, though. "Things have since calmed down at work," Divani has reported, "and I find I have gravitated back to being the person people lean on for emotional support, but at this point it is totally doable."

Make a change

If nothing you are doing has resulted in a shift, your best option may be to leave. Sheung-Li explained: "After two years of this [toxic situation], and at the encouragement of my wife, I saw a therapist. It then became clear to me this work reality was not going to change, this toxic manager was not going anywhere, the stress was eating me alive, and I am the one that needed to change. I did a bunch of things, but I think the key thing I did was I ended up making a lateral move in our company to escape this role and to protect my long-term well-being. It was the best decision I ever made."

Consider therapy

It may sound dramatic, but Sheung-Li's decison to talk to a therapist is a highly useful one. A trained psychologist can help you identify burnout, manage your symptoms of stress, help you learn to say "no," and work through any guilt. Not only can they help you protect yourself from the emotional vagaries of being a toxic handler; they can also assist you in your role. Clinical psychologists themselves are trained to listen to their clients empathetically without taking on their emotions. They can help you build the skills you need to help others without absorbing as much of the emotional burden yourself.

Lastly, here are some things we suggest you avoid. While they seem like good solutions on the surface, they often aren't as helpful as you'd think.

Just venting

While it's good to unburden yourself of your emotions—catharsis *can* reduce aggression—too much venting can actually increase stress levels. You want to move forward, rather than dwelling on problems. And this is as true for those confiding in you as it is for you! When people come to you to vent, consider saying something like, "I hear you! How about we think about what we can change to make this better?"

Going to your boss or HR

Sadly, the role of toxic handler is often underrecognized and underappreciated in organizations, despite its tremendous value. This means that while your boss may want to help, it can be risky for them in many organizational cultures. Similarly, many firms are unlikely to intervene in a toxic situation on behalf of the handler.

Yet toxic handlers are critical to the emotional well-being of organizations and the people in them. If you're a toxic handler, learn to monitor yourself for signs of emotional or physical fatigue—and know how to step away when you need to—so that you can keep doing what you do best.

Sandra L. Robinson is a professor of organizational behavior at the University of British Columbia's Sauder School of Business. **Kira Schabram** is an assistant professor of organizational behavior at the University of Washington's Foster School of Business.

Understand Empathy

CHAPTER 19

What Is Empathy?

by Daniel Goleman

The word "attention" comes from the Latin *attendere*, meaning "to reach toward." This is a perfect definition of focus on others, which is the foundation of empathy and of an ability to build social relationships—the second and third pillars of emotional intelligence (the first is self-awareness).

Executives who can effectively focus on others are easy to recognize. They are the ones who find common ground, whose opinions carry the most weight, and with whom other people want to work. They emerge as natural leaders regardless of organizational or social rank.

The Empathy Triad

We talk about empathy most commonly as a single attribute. But a close look at where leaders are focusing when

Excerpted from "The Focused Leader" in *Harvard Business Review*, December 2013 (product #R0205B)

they exhibit it reveals three distinct kinds of empathy, each important for leadership effectiveness:

- **Cognitive empathy:** the ability to understand another person's perspective.

- **Emotional empathy:** the ability to feel what someone else feels.

- **Empathic concern:** the ability to sense what another person needs from you.

Cognitive empathy enables leaders to explain themselves in meaningful ways—a skill essential to getting the best performance from their direct reports. Contrary to what you might expect, exercising cognitive empathy requires leaders to think about feelings rather than to feel them directly.

An inquisitive nature feeds cognitive empathy. As one successful executive with this trait puts it, "I've always just wanted to learn everything, to understand anybody that I was around—why they thought what they did, why they did what they did, what worked for them and what didn't work." But cognitive empathy is also an outgrowth of self-awareness. The executive circuits that allow us to think about our own thoughts and to monitor the feelings that flow from them let us apply the same reasoning to other people's minds when we choose to direct our attention that way.

Emotional empathy is important for effective mentoring, managing clients, and reading group dynamics. It springs from ancient parts of the brain beneath the cortex—the amygdala, the hypothalamus, the hippocampus, and the orbitofrontal cortex—that allow us to feel fast without thinking deeply. They tune us in by arousing in our bodies the emotional states of others: I literally feel your pain. My brain patterns match up with yours when I listen to you tell a gripping story. As Tania Singer, the director of the social neuroscience department at the Max Planck Institute for Human Cognitive and Brain Sciences, in Leipzig, Germany, says, "You need to understand your own feelings to understand the feelings of others." Accessing your capacity for emotional empathy depends on combining two kinds of attention: a deliberate focus on your own echoes of someone else's feelings and an open awareness of that person's face, voice, and other external signs of emotion. (See the sidebar "When Empathy Needs to Be Learned.")

Empathic concern, which is closely related to emotional empathy, enables you to sense not just how people feel but what they need from you. It's what you want in your doctor, your spouse—and your boss. Empathic concern has its roots in the circuitry that compels parents' attention to their children. Watch where people's eyes go when someone brings an adorable baby into a room, and you'll see this mammalian brain center leaping into action.

Research suggests that as people rise through the ranks, their ability to maintain personal connections suffers.

One neural theory holds that the response is triggered in the amygdala by the brain's radar for sensing danger and in the prefrontal cortex by the release of oxytocin, the chemical for caring. This implies that empathic

WHEN EMPATHY NEEDS TO BE LEARNED

Emotional empathy can be developed. That's the conclusion suggested by research conducted with physicians by Helen Riess, the director of the Empathy and Relational Science Program at Boston's Massachusetts General Hospital. To help the physicians monitor themselves, Riess set up a program in which they learned to focus using deep, diaphragmatic breathing and to cultivate a certain detachment—to watch an interaction from the ceiling, as it were, rather than being lost in their own thoughts and feelings. "Suspending your own involvement to observe what's going on gives you a mindful awareness of the interaction without being completely reactive," says Riess. "You can see if your own physiology is charged up or balanced. You can notice what's transpiring in the situation." If a doctor realizes that she's feeling irritated, for instance, that may be a signal that the patient is bothered too.

Those who are utterly at a loss may be able to prime emotional empathy essentially by faking it until they make it, Riess adds. If you act in a caring way—looking people in the eye and paying attention to their expressions, even when you don't particularly want to—you may start to feel more engaged.

concern is a double-edged feeling. We intuitively experience the distress of another as our own. But in deciding whether we will meet that person's needs, we deliberately weigh how much we value his or her well-being.

Getting this intuition-deliberation mix right has great implications. Those whose sympathetic feelings become too strong may themselves suffer. In the helping professions, this can lead to compassion fatigue; in executives, it can create distracting feelings of anxiety about people and circumstances that are beyond anyone's control. But those who protect themselves by deadening their feelings may lose touch with empathy. Empathic concern requires us to manage our personal distress without numbing ourselves to the pain of others. (See the sidebar "When Empathy Needs to Be Controlled.")

Daniel Goleman is a codirector of the Consortium for Research on Emotional Intelligence in Organizations at Rutgers University, coauthor of *Primal Leadership: Leading with Emotional Intelligence* (Harvard Business Review Press, 2013), and author of *The Brain and Emotional Intelligence: New Insights* and *Leadership: Selected Writings* (More Than Sound, 2011). His latest book is *A Force for Good: The Dalai Lama's Vision for Our World* (Bantam, 2015).

WHEN EMPATHY NEEDS TO BE CONTROLLED

Getting a grip on our impulse to empathize with other people's feelings can help us make better decisions when someone's emotional flood threatens to overwhelm us.

(continued)

(*continued*)

Ordinarily, when we see someone pricked with a pin, our brains emit a signal indicating that our own pain centers are echoing that distress. But physicians learn in medical school to block even such automatic responses. Their attentional anesthetic seems to be deployed by the temporal-parietal junction and regions of the prefrontal cortex, a circuit that boosts concentration by tuning out emotions. That's what is happening in your brain when you distance yourself from others in order to stay calm and help them. The same neural network kicks in when we see a problem in an emotionally overheated environment and need to focus on looking for a solution. If you're talking with someone who is upset, this system helps you understand the person's perspective intellectually by shifting from the heart-to-heart of emotional empathy to the head-to-heart of cognitive empathy.

What's more, some lab research suggests that the appropriate application of empathic concern is critical to making moral judgments. Brain scans have revealed that when volunteers listened to tales of people being subjected to physical pain, their own brain centers for experiencing such pain lit up instantly. But if the story was about psychological suffering, the higher brain centers involved in empathic concern and compassion took longer to activate. Some time is needed to grasp the psychological and moral dimensions of a situation. The more distracted we are, the less we can cultivate the subtler forms of empathy and compassion.

CHAPTER 20

Beyond Empathy: The Power of Compassion

An interview with Daniel Goleman by Andrea Ovans

Two decades before Daniel Goleman first wrote about emotional intelligence in the pages of HBR, he met the Dalai Lama at Amherst College. The Dalai Lama mentioned to the young science journalist for the *New York Times* that he was interested in meeting with scientists. Thus began a long, rich friendship as Goleman became involved over the years in arranging a series of

Adapted from content posted on hbr.org on May 4, 2015, as "What the Dalai Lama Taught Daniel Goleman About Emotional Intelligence" (product #H021KQ)

what he calls "extended dialogues" between the Buddhist spiritual leader and researchers in fields ranging from ecology to neuroscience. On the occasion of his friend's 80th birthday, he was asked to write a book describing the Dalai Lama's compassionate approach to addressing the world's most intractable problems. *A Force for Good: The Dalai Lama's Vision for Our World*, which draws both on Goleman's background in cognitive science and his long relationship with the Dalai Lama, is both an exploration of the science and the power of compassion and a call to action. Curious about the book and about how the Dalai Lama's views on compassion informed Goleman's thinking on emotional intelligence, I caught up with Goleman over the phone. What follows are edited excerpts from our conversation.

HBR: Let's start with some definitions here. What is compassion, as you are describing it? It sounds a lot like empathy, one of the major components of emotional intelligence. Is there a difference?

> **Goleman:** Yes, an important difference. Three kinds of empathy are important to emotional intelligence: *cognitive empathy*—the ability to understand another person's point of view, *emotional empathy*—the ability to feel what someone else feels, and *empathic concern*—the ability to sense what another person needs from you [see chapter 19, "What Is Empathy?"]. Cultivating all three kinds of empathy, which originate in different parts of the brain, is important for building social relationships.

But compassion takes empathy a step further. When you feel compassion, you feel distress when you witness someone else in distress—and because of that you want to help that person.

Why draw this distinction?

Compassion makes the difference between understanding and caring. It's the kind of love that a parent has for a child. Cultivating it more broadly means extending that to the other people in our lives and to people we encounter.

I think that in the workplace, that attitude has a hugely positive effect, whether it's in how we relate to our peers, how we are as a leader, or how we relate to clients and customers. A positive disposition toward another person creates the kind of resonance that builds trust and loyalty and makes interactions harmonious. And the opposite of that—when you do nothing to show that you care—creates distrust and disharmony and causes huge dysfunction at home and in business.

When you put it that way, it's hard to disagree that if you treat people well things would go better than if you don't or that if you cared about them they would care a lot more about you. So why do you think that doesn't just happen naturally? Is it a cultural thing? Or a misplaced confusion about when competition is appropriate?

I think too often there's a muddle in people's thinking that if I'm nice to another person or if I have their interests at heart it means that I don't have my own interests at heart. The pathology of that is, "Well, I'll just care about me and not the other person." And that, of course, is the kind of attitude that leads to lots of problems in the business realm and in the personal realm. But compassion also includes yourself. If we protect ourselves and make sure we're okay—and also make sure the other person is okay—that creates a different framework for working with and cooperating with other people.

Could you give me an example of how that might work in the business world?

There's research that was done on star salespeople and on client managers that found that the lowest level of performance was a kind of "I'm going to get the best deal I can now, and I don't care how this affects the other person" attitude, which means that you might make the sale but that you lose the relationship. But at the top end, the stars were typified by the attitude, "I am working for the client as well as myself. I'm going to be completely straight with them, and I'm going to act as their advisor. If the deal I have is not the best deal they can get I'm going to let them know because that's going to strengthen the relationship, even though I might lose this specific sale." And I think that captures the difference between the "me first" and the "let's all do well" attitude that I'm getting at.

How would we cultivate compassion if we just weren't feeling it?

Neuroscientists have been studying compassion recently, and places like Stanford, Yale, UC Berkeley, and the University of Wisconsin, Madison, among others, have been testing methodologies for increasing compassion. Right now there's a kind of a trend toward incorporating mindfulness into the workplace, and it turns out there's data from the Max Planck Institute showing that enhancing mindfulness does have an effect in brain function but that the circuitry that's affected is not the circuitry for concern or compassion. In other words, there's no automatic boost in compassion from mindfulness alone.

Still, in the traditional methods of meditation that mindfulness in the workplace is based on, the two were always linked, so that you would practice mindfulness in a context in which you'd also cultivate compassion.

Stanford, for example, has developed a program that incorporates secularized versions of methods that have originally come from religious practices. It involves a meditation in which you cultivate an attitude of loving-kindness or of concern, or of compassion, toward people. First you do this for yourself, then for people you love, then for people you just know. And finally you do it for everyone. And this has the effect of priming the circuitry responsible for compassion within the brain so that you are more inclined to act that way when the opportunity arises.

You've remarked that the Dalai Lama is a very distinctive kind of leader. Is there something we could learn as leaders ourselves from his unique form of leadership?

Observing him over the years, and then doing this book for which I interviewed him extensively, and of course being immersed in leadership literature myself, three things struck me.

The first is that he's not beholden to any organization at all. He's not in any business. He's not a party leader. He's a citizen of the world at large. And this has freed him to tackle the largest problems we face. I think that to the extent that a leader is beholden to a particular organization or outcome, that creates a kind of myopia of what's possible and what matters. Focus narrows to the next quarter's results or the next election. He's way beyond that. He thinks in terms of generations and of what's best for humanity as a whole. Because his vision is so expansive, he can take on the largest challenges, rather than small, narrowly defined ones.

So I think there's a lesson here for all of us, which is to ask ourselves if there is something that limits our vision—that limits our capacity to care. And is there a way to enlarge it?

The second thing that struck me is that he gathers information from everywhere. He meets with heads of state, and he meets with beggars. He's getting information from people at every level of society worldwide. This casting a large net lets him understand situations in a very deep way, and he can analyze them in many different ways and come up with solutions that aren't confined by anyone. And I think that's another lesson everyday leaders can take from him.

The third thing would be the scope of his compassion, which I think is an ideal that we could strive for. It's pretty unlimited. He seems to care about everybody and the world at large.

Daniel Goleman is the codirector of the Consortium for Research on Emotional Intelligence in Organizations at Rutgers University, a coauthor of *Primal Leadership: Leading with Emotional Intelligence* (Harvard Business Review Press, 2013), and the author of *The Brain and Emotional Intelligence: New Insights* (More Than Sound, 2011). His latest book is *A Force for Good: The Dalai Lama's Vision for Our World* (Bantam, 2015). **Andrea Ovans** is a former senior editor at *Harvard Business Review*.

Build Your Resilience

CHAPTER 21

Resilience in the Moment

During difficult interactions, you may begin to question your perceptions about yourself. For example, suppose a direct report says, "I didn't attend the meeting because I didn't think you valued my ideas." In response, you wonder to yourself, "Maybe I'm not a competent manager after all."

For many people, the sense that their self-image is being challenged creates intense emotions. These feelings can become overwhelming, making it virtually impossible to converse productively about *any* subject. For this reason, be sure to address feelings about self-image—in yourself and in the other person—during tough conversations.

Adapted from "Address Emotions" in the Harvard ManageMentor topic "Difficult Interactions" (Harvard Business Publishing, 2016, electronic).

Understand Self-Image

Your self-image comes from many different assumptions that you've made about yourself:

- "I'm an effective manager."

- "I'm a good person."

- "I care about my employees."

- "I'm committed to my organization's success."

This set of assumptions may help you meet a need for self-esteem, competence, and appreciation from others. Few people like to view themselves in a negative light—as incompetent, uncaring, or disloyal.

Why Denial Is Common

Many people view self-image from an "either/or" mindset: "I'm either loyal or disloyal" or "I'm either caring or uncaring." Unfortunately, this perspective makes it impossible for people to tolerate criticism and negative feedback from others.

For instance, if a colleague says, "I was really disappointed when you didn't support my proposal," you might conclude, "I can't possibly be a loyal person if I don't support my peer's ideas." If deciding that you're disloyal feels intolerable, you may practice *denial* and shoot back with something like, "I *did* support your proposal."

Other Reactions to Threats

Other reactions to self-image challenges include:

- **Burying the feelings, adopting a detached manner, and resorting to generalizations:** "Let's calm down and establish precise standard operating procedures here."

- **Striking back at the other person defensively:** "Are you calling me a liar?!"

- **Refusing to face the disagreement directly:** "Let's just forget about it and move on."

None of these responses enables you to listen to feedback and make the changes needed to improve the way you interact with others.

Handle Threats to Your Self-Image

Several strategies can help you effectively handle challenges to your self-image:

- **Understand your self-image.** List all the assumptions that influence your perception of yourself. By anticipating that you might experience defensiveness over threats to these particular beliefs, you may be better able to control negative feelings if they do arise.

- **Adopt a "both/and" mindset.** Instead of assuming that you can be, for example, either competent or incompetent, remind yourself that you and others are a mixture of positive and negative. You're likely competent at some things and not so skilled at others.

- **Accept imperfection.** Acknowledge that everyone makes mistakes at times. The key is to learn from them.

HOW TO RESPOND TO CRITICISM

by Peter Bregman

At one point or another, we've all been blindsided by criticism and reacted poorly. I remember once leading a project that I thought was going great—until my two colleagues took me aside to tell me I was being controlling and overbearing. I immediately became defensive. I had trouble listening to them, and I became self-conscious and awkward for the rest of the project.

Surprise criticism about an issue you haven't perceived yourself often has that effect. It emotionally overpowers you. But you can respond more productively. As you listen to the feedback and your adrenaline starts to flow, pause, take a deep breath, and then follow this game plan.

Acknowledge and set aside your feelings. We call it *constructive* criticism, and it usually is, but it can also feel painful, destabilizing, and personal. Notice and acknowledge to yourself the hurt, anger, embarrassment, or insufficiency you might feel. Recognize the feelings, label them as feelings, and then put them aside so the noise doesn't crowd out your hearing.

Also, look beyond the delivery of the criticism. Feedback is hard to give, and your critic may not be skilled at doing it well, but that doesn't mean it's not valuable and insightful. Avoid confusing the package with the message.

Next, don't agree or disagree. Just collect the data. Ask questions. Solicit examples. Recap what you're hearing, all in the spirit of understanding. Let go of the need to respond. That will reduce your defensiveness and give you space to really listen.

Criticism, especially surprise criticism, is useful information about how someone else perceives you. Following these steps will help make sure you can fully understand it and can learn from it.

Peter Bregman is CEO of Bregman Partners, Inc., a global management consulting firm that advises CEOs and their leadership teams.

CHAPTER 22

Cultivate Resilience in Tough Times

A summary of the full-length HBR article "How Resilience Works" by **Diane Coutu**, *highlighting key ideas and examples*

IDEA IN BRIEF

Resilient people possess three defining characteristics:

- They coolly accept the harsh realities facing them.

- They find meaning in terrible times.

Adapted from "How Resilience Works" in *Harvard Business Review*, May 2002 (product #R0205B)

- They have an uncanny ability to improvise, making do with whatever's at hand.

Fortunately, you can learn to be resilient. To cultivate resilience, apply these practices.

Face Down Reality

Instead of slipping into denial to cope with hardship, take a sober, down-to-earth view of the reality of your situation. You'll prepare yourself to act in ways that enable you to endure—training yourself to survive before the fact.

> *Example:* Admiral Jim Stockdale survived being held prisoner and tortured by the Vietcong in part by accepting he could be held for a long time. (He was held for eight years.) Those who didn't make it out of the camps kept optimistically assuming they'd be released on shorter timetables—by Christmas, by Easter, by the Fourth of July. "I think they all died of broken hearts," Stockdale said.

Search for Meaning

When hard times strike, resist any impulse to view yourself as a victim and cry, "Why me?" Rather, devise constructs about your suffering to create meaning for yourself and theirs. You'll build bridges from your present-day ordeal to a fuller, better future. Those bridges will make the present manageable, by removing the sense that the present is overwhelming.

> *Example:* Austrian psychiatrist and Auschwitz survivor Victor Frankl realized that to survive the camp, he had to find some purpose. He did so by imagining

himself giving a lecture after the war on the psychology of the concentration camp to help outsiders understand what he had been through. By creating concrete goals for himself, he rose above the sufferings of the moment.

Continually Improvise

When disaster hits, be inventive. Make the most of what you have, putting resources to unfamiliar uses and imagining possibilities others don't see.

Example: Mike founded a business with his friend Paul, selling educational materials to schools, businesses, and consulting firms. When a recession hit, they lost many core clients. Paul went through a bitter divorce, suffered from depression, and couldn't work. When Mike offered to buy him out, Paul slapped him with a lawsuit claiming Mike was trying to steal the business.

Mike kept the company going any way he could—going into joint ventures to sell English-language training materials to Russian and Chinese competitors, publishing newsletters for clients, and even writing video scripts for competitors. The lawsuit was eventually settled in his favor, and he had a new and much more solid business than the one he started out with.

———————

Diane Coutu is the director of client communications at Banyan Family Business Advisors, headquartered in Cambridge, Massachusetts, and is a former senior editor at *Harvard Business Review*.

CHAPTER 23

Practice Self-Compassion

by Christopher Germer

If a good friend tells you about an ordeal they're facing or a mistake they've made, how do you typically respond? In all likelihood, you'll offer kindness and comfort, perhaps speaking in a warm and soothing tone, and maybe offering a hug to show how much you care. When your friend recovers and the conversation continues, chances are that you'll expand your support by encouraging your friend to take necessary action or try to discover how to steer clear of similar difficulties in the future.

Now reflect for a moment how you might you treat *yourself* when *you* make a big mistake or experience a

---

Adapted from content posted on hbr.org on January 5, 2017, as "To Recover from Failure, Try Some Self-Compassion" (product #H03E32)

setback. It's likely that you'd be much tougher on yourself—that you'd spring to self-criticism ("I'm such an idiot!"), hide in embarrassment or shame ("Ugggh!"), or ruminate for a long time about your perceived shortcomings or bad luck ("Why me? Why did this happen to me?"). When things go wrong in our lives, we tend to become our own worst enemy.

To recover emotionally and get back on your feet, however, there's a different approach you can take: *self-compassion.*

I've been working with mindfulness in my psychotherapy practice for over 30 years. It is a powerful resource that helps us stay present and focused on the task at hand. I've come to realize, however, that a component of mindfulness that is essential for emotional resilience is often overlooked. In particular, when we fail in a big way, we're likely to become engulfed in shame and our sense of self is dismantled. We all know what this feels like—we're unable to think straight, temporarily suspended in time and place, dislocated from our bodies, and uncertain who we really are. Shame has a way of wiping out the very observer who is needed to be mindful of our situation.

What does it take to rescue yourself and begin to address the situation in an effective manner? You need to treat yourself with the same kindness and support as you'd provide for a dear friend.

A substantial and growing body of research shows that this self-compassion is closely associated with emotional resilience, including the ability to soothe ourselves, recognize our mistakes and learn from them, and motivate ourselves to succeed. Self-compassion is also consistently correlated with a wide range of measures of emotional well-being such as optimism, life satisfaction, autonomy, and wisdom, and with reduced anxiety, depression, stress, and feelings of shame.[1]

To achieve these benefits, self-compassion must include three components, according to my colleague and pioneering self-compassion researcher, Kristin Neff:

- **Mindfulness:** Awareness of what's going on in the present moment. To be kind to ourselves, first we need to *know* that we're struggling *while* we're struggling. It also helps to name the emotions we're feeling in tricky situations and to ground ourselves in the here and now (sensations, sounds, sights). These are all skills associated with mindfulness that make space for a compassionate response.

- **Common humanity:** Knowing we're not alone. Most of us tend to hide in shame when things go really wrong in our lives, or we hide from *ourselves* through distraction or with a few stiff drinks. The antidote is recognizing our common humanity— understanding that many others would feel the same way in similar situations, and that we're not the only ones who suffer in life.

- **Self-kindness:** A kind and warm-hearted response to ourselves. This can take many forms, such as a gentle hand over the heart, validating how we feel, talking to ourselves in an encouraging manner, or by a simple act of kindness such as drinking a cup of tea or listening to music.

When we feel threatened, our nervous system is awash in adrenaline and thus goes into overdrive. When we're in this state, showing ourselves care and kindness is usually the last thing we're inclined to do. When we experience positive, warm connections, however, our system releases oxytocin instead, a feel-good hormone that downregulates the effects of adrenaline. Taking a mindful pause and then bringing kindness to ourselves seems to activate our innate caregiving system and the calming effect of oxytocin, allowing the mind to clear and giving us a chance to take rational steps to resolve the issue.

Even though self-compassion is not the default option for most of us when things go wrong, anyone can learn to do it. Neff has developed an exercise you can use in everyday life when you need self-compassion the most—the Self-Compassion Break (see the sidebar "Self-Compassion Break")—which is based on the three components of self-compassion described above. (This is just one exercise we offer as part of our empirically supported Mindful Self-Compassion training program.)

SELF-COMPASSION BREAK

When you notice that you're under stress or are emotionally upset, see if you can locate where the emotional discomfort resides your body. Where do you feel it the most? Then say to yourself, slowly:

1. ***"This is a moment of struggle."*** That's mindfulness. See if you can find your own words, such as:

   - "This hurts."
   - "This is tough."
   - "Ouch!"

2. ***"Struggle is a part of living."*** That's common humanity. Other options include:

   - "Other people feel this way."
   - "I'm not alone."
   - "We all struggle in our lives."

Now, put your hands over your heart, or wherever it feels soothing, sensing the warmth and gentle touch of your hands, and say to yourself:

3. ***"May I be kind to myself. May I give myself what I need."*** Perhaps there are more specific words that you might need to hear right now, such as:

   - "May I accept myself as I am."
   - "May I learn to accept myself as I am."
   - "May I be safe."
   - "May I be strong."
   - "May I forgive myself."

(continued)

SELF-COMPASSION BREAK

(*continued*)

If you're having trouble finding the right language, it can help to imagine what you might say to a close friend struggling with that same difficulty. Can you say something similar to yourself, letting the words roll gently through your mind?

Consider the following example of the Self-Compassion Break in action: Your boss gave you a stretch assignment to lead a large and critical project. The project was a great success, due in large part to your skillful leadership, and you believe you demonstrated that you're ready for a promotion. But when you raise the idea with your boss, she laughs dismissively and changes the subject. Livid with anger, you retreat from the conversation, asking yourself why you bothered to work so hard in the first place, since you would never be recognized for it. *Of course* your boss wasn't going to support you, or even notice—she just wanted someone to do the heavy lifting to promote her own selfish agenda. Or maybe you're hopelessly out of touch and your performance really wasn't as good as you thought it was? When we're in the grip of strong emotions, our minds run wild.

As a savvy businessperson, you might think that this would be the perfect moment to advocate for yourself if it were only possible to make a balanced, compelling case for your promotion. But without a moment of self-compassion, your emotional reactivity is likely to stand in your way—you'd put your anger on display instead of showing off your leadership skills, or you'd let self-doubt eat at your resolve to see the discussion through to an acceptable conclusion.

How do you activate self-compassion in the heat of the moment? Begin by acknowledging how you feel; for example, recognizing that you might still feel angry ("She's terrible, and I hate her"), see yourself as the victim ("She made me go through all of that—for what?!"), or doubt yourself ("Maybe she's right—maybe I don't deserve a promotion—I didn't do that great a job after all").

Next, acknowledge that others would probably have similar feelings in this situation: requesting a promotion after you've expanded your skills and taken on more responsibility is a reasonable thing to do, and your emotional reaction to the rejection of that request is not out of line. Consider any examples you know of others in similar situations—perhaps Rob in the finance department told you last year that his promotion was also denied and you noticed how angry he was and how he doubted his own worth. You are not alone.

Finally, express kindness to yourself: What would you say to a friend in your shoes? Perhaps you'd say, "It's rough being taken for granted." "Whatever comes of it, that project *was* a huge success—look at the numbers." Also think about how you care for yourself already. Do you go for a run, pet your dog, call a friend? If you do that when you're suffering, that's self-compassion.

Once you've shifted your frame of mind from a threat state to self-compassion, you're likely find yourself calmer and in a place that you can sit down and write a thoughtful and persuasive proposal about your promotion—one that builds on your project success and exhibits your leadership potential under stress.

Lastly, a warning: Many people dismiss self-compassion because they think it flies in the face of their ambition or hard self-driving attitude—qualities that they feel have made them successful. But being self-compassionate doesn't imply that you shouldn't be ambitious or push yourself to succeed. Rather it's about *how* you motivate yourself. Instead of using a whip—motivating yourself with blame and harsh self-criticism—self-compassion motivates like a good coach, with encouragement, kindness, and support. It's a simple reversal of the Golden Rule—learning to treat *ourselves* as we naturally treat others in need—with kindness, warmth, and respect.

Christopher Germer is a clinical psychologist and part-time lecturer on psychiatry at Harvard Medical School. He is a co-developer of the Mindful Self-Compassion (MSC) program, author of *The Mindful Path to Self-Compassion*, co-editor of *Mindfulness and Psychotherapy*, and *Wisdom and Compassion in Psychotherapy*, and a founding faculty member of the Institute for Meditation and Psychotherapy and the Center for Mindfulness and Compassion, Cambridge Health Alliance/Harvard Medical School.

NOTE

1. See, for example: L. K. Barnard and J. F. Curry, "Self-Compassion: Conceptualizations, Correlates, and Interventions," *Review of General*

Psychology 15, no. 4 (2011): 289–303; K. D. Neff, S. S. Rude, and K. Kirkpatrick, "An Examination of Self-Compassion in Relation to Positive Psychological Functioning and Personality Traits," *Journal of Research in Personality* 41 (2007): 908–916; F. Raes, "The Effect of Self-Compassion on the Development of Depression Symptoms in a Non-clinical Sample," *Mindfulness* 2 (2011): 33–36; D. L. Zabelina and M. D. Robinson, "Don't Be So Hard on Yourself: Self-Compassion Facilitates Creative Originality Among Self-Judgmental Individuals," *Creativity Research Journal* 22 (2010): 288–293; E. Schanche et al., "The Relationship Between Activating Affects, Inhibitory Affects, and Self-Compassion in Patients with Cluster C Personality Disorders," *Psychotherapy* 48, no. 3 (2011): 293–303.

CHAPTER 24

Don't Endure; Recharge

by Shawn Achor and Michelle Gielan

As constant travelers and parents of a two-year-old, we sometimes fantasize about how much work we could do if we could just get on a plane, undistracted by phones, friends, or *Finding Nemo*. And so in advance of a trip, we race to get all our groundwork done: packing, going through TSA, doing a last-minute work call, calling each other, boarding. But then when we try to have that amazing in-flight work session, we find that we get nothing done. Even worse, after refreshing our email or reading the same studies over and over, we are too exhausted when we land to soldier on with the emails that have inevitably still piled up.

Adapted from content posted on hbr.org on June 24, 2016, as "Resilience Is About How You Recharge, Not How You Endure" (product #H02Z3O)

Why can't we be tougher—more resilient and determined in our work—so we can accomplish all of the goals we set for ourselves? Through our current research, we have come to realize that the problem comes from a cultural misunderstanding of what it means to be resilient, and the resulting impact of overworking.

As a society, we often associate "resilience" and "grit" with a militaristic, "tough" approach to our work. We imagine a Marine slogging through the mud, a boxer going one more round, or a football player picking himself up off the turf for one more play. We believe that the longer we tough it out, the tougher we are, and therefore the more successful we will be.

However, this entire conception is scientifically inaccurate. In fact what's holding back our ability to be resilient and successful is the lack of any kind of recovery period. Resilience is defined as the ability to quickly bounce back from stressful situations—no matter what problems are thrown at us, we continually get back up, ready for the next one. But even for the most resilient person, getting ready doesn't happen instantly. It is a process—and an important one. Research has found that there is a direct correlation between lack of recovery and increased incidence of health and safety problems. And lack of recovery—whether it disrupts our sleep with thoughts of work or keeps us in continuous cognitive arousal as we obsessively watch our phones—is costing our companies $62 billion a year (that's *billion*, not million) in lost productivity.[1]

Misconceptions about resilience as nonstop activity and energy are often bred into us from an early age.

For instance, parents might praise the resilience of their high school student who stays up until 3 a.m. to finish a science fair project. But when that exhausted student drives to school, his impaired driving poses risks for himself and others; at school, he doesn't have the cognitive resources to do well on his English test and has lower self-control with his friends; and at home, he is moody with his parents.

The bad habits we learn when we're young only magnify when we hit the workforce. In a study released last month, researchers from Norway found that 7.8% of Norwegians have become workaholics, where *workaholism* is defined as "being overly concerned about work, driven by an uncontrollable work motivation, and investing so much time and effort to work that it impairs other important life areas."[2] And in fact that drive can backfire in the very area for which we're sacrificing ourselves: In her excellent book *The Sleep Revolution: Transforming Your Life, One Night at a Time*, Arianna Huffington wrote, "We sacrifice sleep in the name of productivity, but ironically our loss of sleep, despite the extra hours we spend at work, adds up to 11 days of lost productivity per year per worker, or about $2,280."[3]

The key to resilience is *not* working really hard all the time. It is actually found in the time that we stop working and recover. Ideally, we need to create cycles for ourselves in which we work hard, then stop and recover, and then work again.

This conclusion is based on biology. *Homeostasis*, a fundamental biological concept, is the ability of the body to continuously restore and sustain its own well-being.

When the body is out of alignment and therefore in a state of stress or exhaustion from overworking, we waste a vast amount of mental and physical resources trying to return to balance before we can move forward. As Jim Loehr and Tony Schwartz have written in *The Power of Full Engagement*, the more time you spend in the performance zone, the more time you need in the recovery zone; otherwise you risk burnout.

And if, instead of taking a break, you muster your resources to continue to "try hard," you need to burn ever more energy in order to overcome your currently low arousal level, which only exacerbates your exhaustion. It's a vicious downward spiral.

But the more imbalanced we become due to overworking, the more value there is in activities that allow us to return to a state of balance.

So what are those activities that allow us to return to homeostasis and thereby increase our resilience? Most people assume that if you stop doing a task like answering emails or writing a paper, that your brain will naturally recover, so that when you start again later in the day or the next morning, you'll have your energy back. But stopping work doesn't mean you're actually recovering: If after work you lie around on the couch and check your phone and get riled up by political commentary, or get stressed thinking about decisions about how to renovate your home, your brain has not received a break from high mental arousal states. And surely everyone reading this has occasionally lain in bed for hours, unable to fall asleep because their brain is thinking about work, even if they don't have a device in hand. If you're in bed for eight hours, you may have rested, but you can still feel exhausted the next day. That's because rest and recovery are not the same thing.

If you're trying to build resilience at work, you need adequate internal and external recovery periods. As researchers F. R. H. Zijlstra, M. Cropley, and L. W. Rydstedt wrote in a 2014 paper: "Internal recovery refers to the shorter periods of relaxation that take place within the frames of the workday or the work setting in the form of short scheduled or unscheduled breaks, by shifting attention or changing to other work tasks when the mental or physical resources required for the initial task are temporarily depleted or exhausted. External recovery refers to actions that take place outside of work—e.g., in the free time between the workdays, and during weekends, holidays or vacations."[4]

There are four main researched ways to increase your resilience. First, start by deliberately opening a space for recovery to happen. We've worked with several companies that tout the benefits of investing in employee well-being, but fail to create tangible results because they don't carve out time for their workers to devote part of their workday to those rejuvenating activities. Adding more activities to an already full plate of work increases the stress load.

Second, it is crucial that you take *all* of your paid time off. As we described in a previous HBR article entitled "The Data-Driven Case for Vacation," taking your days off not only gives you recovery periods to recharge, but in fact significantly raises your productivity and the likelihood of promotion.

Third, while it might sound counterintuitive, it is possible to use technology to limit tech use while building internal recovery periods into your daily routine. The average person turns on their phone 150 times every day.[5] If every distraction took only 1 minute (which would be seriously optimistic), that would account for 2.5 hours of every day. In her upcoming book *The Future of Happiness*, based on her work at Yale Business School, Amy Blankson suggests downloading the Instant or Moment apps to see how many times *you* turn on your phone each day; using the app reminds you to make a choice in those moments when you grab your phone—and choose to stay away. You can also use apps like Offtime or Unplugged to create tech-free zones by strategically scheduling automatic airplane modes. In addition, you can take a cognitive break every 90 minutes to recharge your batteries. Try to not have lunch at your desk, but instead spend time outside or with your friends—*not* talking about work.

Fourth, now that you have carved out time for rejuvenation, it's time to engage in an activity or two that make you feel happy and replenished. Take the pressure off and just do something for the fun of it! Go on a walk or run, call and old friend, meditate by watching your breath go in and out for five minutes, try a new recipe, or do something nice for someone else. Choose to do something that makes you feel alive, gives you a mental break from work, and keeps you fully engaged the whole time. Not only does spending your time this way help you come back stronger, oftentimes these activities are more memorable in the long run.

As for us, we've started using our plane time as a work-free zone, and thus as time to dip into the recovery phase. The results have been fantastic. We are usually tired already by the time we get on a plane, and the cramped space and spotty internet connection make work more challenging. Now, instead of swimming upstream, we relax, meditate, sleep, watch movies, journal, or listen to entertaining podcasts. And when we get off the plane, instead of being depleted, we feel rejuvenated and ready to return to the performance zone.

Shawn Achor is *New York Times* best-selling author of *The Happiness Advantage* and *Before Happiness*. His TED talk is one of the most popular, with over 14 million views. He has lectured or researched at over a third of the *Fortune* 100 and in 50 countries, as well as for the NFL, NASA, and the White House. He is leading a series of courses on "21 Days to Inspire Positive Change" with the Oprah Winfrey Network. **Michelle Gielan**, a national CBS News anchor turned UPenn positive psychology researcher, is the best-selling author of *Broadcasting Happiness*. She is partnered with Arianna Huffington to research how a solution-focused mindset fuels success, and shares her research at organizations including Google, American Express, and Boston Children's Hospital. Michelle is the host of the *Inspire Happiness* program on PBS.

NOTES

1. J. K. Sluiter, "The Influence of Work Characteristics on the Need for Recovery and Experienced Health: A Study on Coach Drivers,"

Ergonomics 42, no. 4 (1999): 573–583; and American Academy of Sleep Medicine, "Insomnia Costing U.S. Workforce $63.2 Billion a Year in Lost Productivity," *ScienceDaily*, September 2, 2011.

2. C. S. Andreassen et al., "The Relationships Between Workaholism and Symptoms of Psychiatric Disorders: A Large-Scale Cross-Sectional Study," *PLoS One* 11, no. 5 (2016): e0152978.

3. Ronald C. Kessler et al., "Insomnia and the Performance of US Workers: Results from the America Insomnia Survey," *Sleep* 34, no. 9 (2011): 1161–1171.

4. F. R. H. Zijlstra et al., "From Recovery to Regulation: An Attempt to Reconceptualize 'Recovery from Work'" (special issue paper) (Hoboken, NJ: John Wiley & Sons, 2014), 244.

5. J. Stern, "Cellphone Users Check Phones 150x/Day and Other Internet Fun Facts," *Good Morning America*, May 29, 2013.

CHAPTER 25

How Resilient Are You?

by Manfred F. R. Kets de Vries

We all face setbacks from time to time, and the ability to bounce back stronger than before is something we envy in others. So how can we develop that ability in ourselves?

A large body of research shows that resilient people are generally strong in three areas: challenge, control, and commitment. They accept that change, not stability, is the norm; they believe they can influence events in their lives; and they are engaged with the world around them.

This test will help you assess your strengths and weaknesses in these areas and provide feedback on ways to improve.

Adapted from material originally published on hbr.org on January 20, 2015

Circle your reaction to each statement, then follow the instructions below to score yourself.

Challenge

1. You're told that you won't be getting the promotion you sought, because another candidate is more qualified.

   a. Although you are upset, you say nothing.
   b. You acknowledge that you are disappointed and request a fuller explanation.
   c. You ask what you need to do to improve your chances for advancement in the future.

2. You learn that your company will be opening an office in Beijing. Succeeding in that market would be difficult, but you know that you have the right experience to lead the office.

   a. You consider the risks and decide not to pursue the opportunity.
   b. You discuss the pros and cons with some of the people in your network.
   c. You throw your hat into the ring.

3. A major client tells you that a contract you worked hard to win has been given to a competitor.

   a. You tell your team that you made every effort to land the client.
   b. You put the setback out of your mind, accepting that some factors in the client's decision were beyond your control.

    c. You reflect on the experience, realizing that you now have a much better understanding of how to deal with this client in the future.

Control

4. You overhear an unflattering conversation about yourself.

   a. You pretend it doesn't bother you.
   b. You remind yourself that the speakers don't know you very well.
   c. You approach the speakers calmly and express your desire to understand why they see you that way.

5. Your boss comes to you on Friday afternoon with an emergency: He wants to meet with a client on Monday morning and needs you to prepare a feasibility study first. You have a family camping trip planned for the weekend.

   a. You accept the assignment, not mentioning your weekend plans.
   b. You mention the camping trip but agree to the assignment after your boss emphasizes its importance.
   c. You tell your boss that you have made a commitment to your family and ask if he can schedule the meeting for Tuesday instead.

6. Work has become increasingly stressful. There are too many deadlines, too many requests, too many late nights.

     a. You tell yourself, "This, too, shall pass."

     b. You try to give some of your work to a colleague.

     c. You request a vacation or a leave of absence to recharge.

Commitment

7. Your best friend says that he is worried about your health and suggests that you join his fitness club.

     a. You say, "No, thanks. I'm fine."

     b. You agree that the fitness club is a good idea and make a note in your calendar to look into it.

     c. You take his concern to heart and arrange to visit the club together.

8. Your company's subsidiary in Africa requests financial and technical support for a high school in the region. Although there would be no immediate monetary benefit to the firm, this is a valuable opportunity to build a reputation as a socially responsible employer.

     a. You decline the request on cost grounds.

     b. You agree to give the matter serious consideration.

     c. You give your consent and call a friend at the World Bank for suggestions on how to launch the initiative.

9. Early in your career you had set a goal to become general manager at a *Fortune* 1000 company by

age 50. The clock is ticking: You're 48, and you're a division head.

a. You accept your current role and decide to make the best of it.
b. You continue striving for advancement but lower your ambitions a bit.
c. You figure out a way to reach your goal.

Score Yourself

For each area, record the number of each answer below and add up your total score for that area.

Challenge

\# of a _____ =

\# of b _____ x 2 =

\# of c _____ x 3 =

Total = _____ = Challenge Score

If you had a high challenge score (7–9):

You turn difficult events to your advantage and view setbacks as learning opportunities. You have positive relationships with others.

If you had a low challenge score (1–6):

You need to work on turning difficult events to your advantage and reframing them in a constructive light. If you experience setbacks in the process, regard them as learning opportunities, not failures. Remember the importance of positive relationships with others.

Control

of a _____   =

# of b _____ x 2 =

# of c _____ x 3 =

       Total =   = Control Score

If you had a high control score (7–9):

You can distinguish between things you can and can't control, and you deal with emotionally difficult problems proactively. You see things in perspective and know how to set boundaries.

If you had a low control score (1–6):

Work on distinguishing between things you can and can't control, perhaps with the help of an executive coach or a therapist. Try to deal with emotionally difficult problems proactively. Use humor to "roll with the punches." Set boundaries in both your professional life and your personal life to avoid burnout. Delegate more responsibilities to your direct reports.

Commitment

of a _____   =

# of b _____ x 2 =

# of c _____ x 3 =

       Total =   = Commitment Score

If you had a high commitment score (7–9):

You pursue goals that are meaningful to you and maintain positive relationships with people who matter to you. You recognize the importance of health and balance and have an active life outside of work.

If you had a low commitment score (1–6):

Clarify what is important to you and pursue those activities. Make an effort to spend time with people who are meaningful in your life. Develop healthy habits, including daily exercise, regular sleep, and relaxation techniques. Don't ignore problems.

To take this assessment online and compare your results to those of other HBR readers, visit https://hbr .org/2015/01/assessment-how-resilient-are-you.

Manfred F. R. Kets de Vries is the Distinguished Professor of Leadership Development and Organizational Change at INSEAD in France, Singapore, and Abu Dhabi. His most recent book is *Riding the Leadership Roller Coaster: An Observer's Guide* (Palgrave Macmillan, 2016).

Developing Emotional Intelligence on Your Team

CHAPTER 26

How to Help Someone Develop Emotional Intelligence

by Annie McKee

It's easy to point fingers at those in the office who lack basic self-awareness or social skill. Whether clueless colleagues or brutish bosses, these people make life challenging for the rest of us, ruining the dynamic of work teams and shattering productivity and morale. But in fact most of us can stand to improve our emotional intelligence. Even those of us who are adept extroverts can

---

Adapted from content posted on hbr.org on April 24, 2015 (product #H0216Z)

learn how to become more empathetic; those who are kind givers can learn to be more persuasive.

As a manager, it's up to you to develop the emotional intelligence of your direct reports—whether they are socially awkward, downright nasty, or simply looking to become more influential. In doing so, you'll help them grow in their careers—and make your workplace a healthier, happier, more productive place to be.

Here's the problem: Emotional intelligence is difficult to develop because it is linked to psychological development and neurological pathways created over an entire lifetime (to learn more, see Daniel Goleman's book *The Brain and Emotional Intelligence: New Insights*). It takes a lot of effort to change long-standing habits of human interaction—not to mention foundational competencies like self-awareness and emotional self-control. People need to be invested in changing their behavior and developing their emotional intelligence, or it just doesn't happen. What this means in practice is that you don't have even a remote chance of changing someone's emotional intelligence unless *they* want to change.

Most of us assume that people will change their behavior when told to do so by a person with authority (you, the manager). For complicated change and development, however, it is clear that people don't *sustain* change when promised incentives like good assignments or a better office.[1] And when threatened or punished, they get downright ornery and behave really badly. Carrot-and-stick performance management processes and the behaviorist approach on which they are based are deeply flawed; yet most of us start (and end) there, even in the most innovative organizations.

What *does* work is:

First, helping people find a deep and very personal vision of their own future.

Then, helping them see how their current ways of operating might need a bit of work if that future is to be realized.

These are the first two steps in Richard Boyatzis's *intentional change* theory—which we've been testing with leaders for years. According to Boyatzis—and backed up by our work with leaders—here's how people really can begin and sustain change on complex abilities linked to emotional intelligence:

First, find the dream

If you're coaching an employee, you must *first* help them discover what's important in life. Only then can you move on to aspects of work that are important to them. Help your employee craft a clear and compelling vision of a future that includes powerful and positive relationships with family, friends, and coworkers. Notice that I'm talking about *coaching*, not *managing*, your employee. There's a big difference.

Next, find out what's really going on

What's the current state of your employee's emotional intelligence? Once people have a powerful dream to draw strength from, they're strong enough to take the heat—to find out the truth. If you are now truly coaching, you're trusted and your employee will listen to you. Still, that's probably not enough. You will want to find a way to gather input from others, either through a 360-degree feedback instrument like the ESCI (Emotional and Social Competency Inventory), or a Leadership Self-Study process (as described in our book, *Becoming a Resonant Leader*), which gives you the chance to talk directly to trusted friends about their emotional intelligence and other skills.

Finally, craft a gap analysis and a learning plan

Note that I did not say "performance management plan," or even "development plan." A learning plan is different in that it charts a direct path from the personal vision to what must be learned over time to get there—to actual skill development.

Learning goals are *big*. Take, for example, one executive I know. Talented though he was, his distinct lack of caring about the people around him had placed him in danger of being fired. He wanted what he wanted—and watch out if you were in his way. He couldn't seem to change until it finally dawned on him that his bulldozer style was playing out at home too, with his children. That didn't fit at all with his dream of a happy, close-knit family who would live close to each other throughout their lives. So, with a dream in hand and the ugly reality rearing its head at work and at home, he decided to work on developing empathy. As a learning goal, empathy is one of the toughest and most important competencies to develop. The capacity for emotional and cognitive empathy is laid down early in life, and then reinforced over many years. This exec had a good foundation for empathy in childhood, but intense schooling and a stint at an up-or-out management consulting firm had driven it out of him. He needed to relearn how to read people and care about them. He was able to succeed—yes, it took a good while, but he did it.

This sounds like a lot of hard work for your employee, and it can be. Here's where a final important piece of the theory comes into play. They—and you—can't do it alone. People need people—kind and supportive people—when embarking on a journey of self-development. Are you there for your employees? Do you help them find other supporters, in addition to yourself, who will help when their confidence wanes or when they experience inevitable setbacks?

Developing one's emotional intelligence can make the difference between success and failure in life and in work. If you're the one responsible for people's contributions to the team and your organization, you are actually on the hook to try to help those (many) people who are emotional-intelligence-challenged, deficient, and dangerous. It's your job.

But what if you're not the boss? You can still make a difference with colleagues. All of the same rules apply to how people change. You just need to find a different entry point. In my experience, that entry begins with you creating a safe space and establishing trust. Find something to like about these people and let them know it. Give them credit where credit is due, and then some (most of these folks are pretty insecure). Be kind. In other words, use your emotional intelligence to help them get ready to work on theirs.

And finally, if none of this works, these "problem people" don't belong on your team—or maybe even in your organization. If you're a manager, that's when it's time to help them move on with dignity.

Annie McKee is a senior fellow at the University of Pennsylvania and the director of the PennCLO Executive Doctoral Program. She is the author of *Primal Leadership* (with Daniel Goleman and Richard Boyatzis), as well as *Resonant Leadership* and *Becoming a Resonant Leader*. Her new book, *How to Be Happy at Work*, is forthcoming from Harvard Business Review Press in September 2017.

NOTE

1. "What Motivates Us?" interview between Daniel Pink and Katherine Bell, *HBR Ideacast* (podcast), February 10, 2010.

CHAPTER 27

Handling Emotional Outbursts on Your Team

by Liane Davey

Do you have a crier on your team—you know, the one with tissue-thin skin who expresses frustration, sadness, or worry through tears? Maybe you have a screamer, a table pounder who is aggressively invested in every decision. These kinds of emotional outbursts are not just uncomfortable; they can hijack your team, stalling productivity and limiting innovation.

Adapted from content originally posted on hbr.org on April 24, 2015, as "Handling Emotional Outbursts on Your Team."

Don't allow an emotional person to postpone, dilute, or drag out an issue that the business needs you to resolve. Instead, take the outburst for what it is: a communication. Emotions are clues that the issue you are discussing is touching on something the person values or believes strongly in. So look at outbursts as giving you three sets of information: emotional data; factual or intellectual data; and motives, values, and beliefs.

We get stuck when we only focus on the first two—emotions and facts. It's easy to do. When someone starts yelling, for instance, you might think he's mad (emotion) because his project has just been defunded (fact). And many managers stop there, because they find feelings uncomfortable or aren't sure how to deal with them. That's why the first step is to become more self-aware by questioning your mindset around emotions. There are several myths that often get in a team leader's way:

Myth #1: There is no place for emotion in the workplace. If you have humans in the workplace, you're going to have emotions too. Ignoring, stifling, or invalidating them will only drive the toxic issues underground. This outdated notion is one reason people resort to passive-aggressive behavior: Emotions will find their outlet; the choice is whether it's out in the open or in the shadows.

Myth #2: We don't have time to talk about people's feelings. Do you have time for backroom dealings and subterfuge? Do you have time to reopen decisions? Do you have time for failed implementations? Avoiding the emotional issues at the outset will only delay their impact. And when people don't feel heard, their feelings amplify until you have something really destructive to deal with.

Myth #3: Emotions will skew our decision making. Emotions are already affecting your decision making. The choice is whether you want to be explicit about how (and how much) of a role they play or whether you want to leave them as unspoken biases.

With your beliefs in check, you'll be better able to get beyond the emotion and facts to the values the person holds that are being compromised or violated. This is critical because your criers and screamers are further triggered when they don't feel understood. The key is to have a discussion that includes facts, feelings, *and* values. People will feel heard and the emotion will usually dissipate. Then you can focus on making the best business decision possible.

Here's how.

Spot the emotion. If you wait until the emotion is in full bloom, it will be difficult to manage. Instead, watch for the telltale signs that something is causing concern. The most important signals will come from incongruence between what someone is saying and what their body language is telling you. When you notice someone is withdrawing eye contact or getting red in the face, acknowledge what you see: *"Steve, you've stopped midsentence a couple of times now. What's going on for you?"*

Listen. Listen carefully to the response, both to what is said and what you can infer about facts, feelings, and values. You will pick up emotions in language, particularly in extreme words or words that are repeated: *"We have a $2 million budget shortfall and it's our fourth meeting sitting around having a lovely intellectual discussion!"* Body language will again provide clues. Angry (leaning in, clenched jaw or fists) looks very different from discouraged (dropping eye contact, slumping) or dismissive (rolling eyes, turning away).

Ask questions. When you see or hear the emotional layer, stay calm, keep your tone level, and ask a question to draw the person out and get them talking about values: *"I get the sense you're frustrated. What's behind your frustration?"* Listen to their response and then go one layer further by testing a hypothesis: *"Is it possible that you're frustrated because we're placing too much weight on the people impact of the decision and you think we need to focus only on what's right for the business?"*

Resolve it. If your hypothesis is right, you'll probably see relief. The person might even express their pleasure: *"Yes, exactly!"* You can sum it up: *"We've talked about closing the Cleveland office for two years and you're frustrated because you believe that the right decision for the business is obvious."* You've now helped them articulate the values they think should be guiding the decision. The team will now be clear on why they are disagreeing. Three people might jump in, all talking at once: *"We are talking about* *people who have given their lives to this organization!" "Here we go again . . ."* Use the same process to reveal the opposing points of view.

Once everyone is working with the same three data sets—facts, emotions, and values—you will be clear what you need to solve for—in this case, *"How will we weigh the financial necessity against the impact on people?"* Although taking the time to draw out the values might seem slow at first, you'll see that issues actually get resolved faster. And ironically, as you validate emotions, over time people will tend to be less emotional because it's often the suppression of emotions or attempts to cobble together facts to justify those emotions that was causing irrational behavior.

If you're leading a high-performing team, you'd better be ready to deal with uncomfortable, messy, complex emotions. If there's a situation you have failed to address because of an emotional team member, spend some time thinking about how you will approach it and then go have the conversation. Today. You can't afford to wait any longer.

Liane Davey is the cofounder of 3COze Inc. She is the author of *You First: Inspire Your Team to Grow Up, Get Along, and Get Stuff Done* and a coauthor of *Leadership Solutions: The Pathway to Bridge the Leadership Gap.* Follow her on Twitter @LianeDavey.

CHAPTER 28

How to Manage Your Emotional Culture

by Sigal Barsade and Olivia A. O'Neill

When people talk about "corporate culture," they're typically referring to *cognitive* culture: the shared *intellectual* values, norms, artifacts, and assumptions that serve as a guide for the group to thrive. Cognitive culture sets the tone for how employees think and behave at work—for instance, how customer-focused, innovative, team-oriented, or competitive they are or should be.

Cognitive culture is undeniably important to an organization's success. But it's only part of the story. The

---

Adapted from "Manage Your Emotional Culture" in *Harvard Business Review*, January 2016 (product #R0601C)

other critical part is what we call the group's *emotional* culture: the shared *affective* values, norms, artifacts, and assumptions that govern which emotions people have and express at work and which ones they are better off suppressing. Though the key distinction here is thinking versus feeling, the two types of culture are also transmitted differently: Cognitive culture is often conveyed verbally, whereas emotional culture tends to be conveyed through nonverbal cues such as body language and facial expression.

In our research over the past decade, we have found that emotional culture influences employee satisfaction, burnout, teamwork, and even hard measures such as financial performance and absenteeism. Countless empirical studies show the significant impact of emotions on how people perform on tasks, how engaged and creative they are, how committed they are to their organizations, and how they make decisions. Positive emotions are consistently associated with better performance, quality, and customer service—this holds true across roles and industries and at various organizational levels. On the flip side (with certain short-term exceptions), negative emotions such as group anger, sadness, fear, and the like usually lead to negative outcomes, including poor performance and high turnover.

So when managers ignore emotional culture, they're glossing over a vital part of what makes people—and organizations—tick. They may understand its importance in theory but can still shy away from emotions at work. Leaders expect to influence how people think and behave on the job, but they may feel ill-equipped to understand and actively manage how employees feel and express their emotions at work. Or they may regard doing so as irrelevant, not part of their job, or unprofessional.

Emotional Cultures in Action

Nearly 30 years ago, the social psychologist Phil Shaver and his colleagues found that people can reliably distinguish among 135 emotions. But understanding the most basic ones—joy, love, anger, fear, sadness—is a good place to start for any leader trying to manage an emotional culture. Here are a few examples to illustrate how these emotions can play out in organizations.

A Culture of Joy

Let's begin with one that's often clearly articulated and actively reinforced by management—above the surface and easy to spot. Vail Resorts recognizes that cultivating joy among employees helps customers have fun too, which matters a lot in the hospitality business. It also gives the organization an edge in retaining top talent in an extremely competitive industry. "Have fun" is listed as a company value and modeled by Vail's CEO, Rob Katz—who, for instance, had ice water dumped on his head during a corporate ALS Ice Bucket Challenge and then jumped fully clothed into a pool. About 250 executives and other employees followed his lead.

This playful spirit at the top permeates Vail. Management tactics, special outings, celebrations, and rewards all support the emotional culture. Resort managers consistently model joy and prescribe it for their teams.

During the workday, they give out pins when they notice employees spontaneously having fun or helping others enjoy their jobs. Rather than asking people to follow standardized customer service scripts, they tell everyone to "go out there and have fun." Mark Gasta, the company's chief people officer, says he regularly sees ski-lift operators dancing, making jokes, doing "whatever it takes to have fun and entertain the guest" while ensuring a safe experience on the slopes. On a day-to-day basis, Vail encourages employees to collaborate because, as Gasta points out, "leaving people out is not fun." At an annual ceremony, a Have Fun award goes to whoever led that year's best initiative promoting fun at work. The resort also fosters off-the-job joy with "first tracks" (first access to the ski slopes for employees), adventure trips, and frequent social gatherings.

All this is in service to an emotional culture that makes intuitive sense. (Joy at a ski resort? Of course.) But now consider an organization where the demand for joy wasn't immediately visible. When we surveyed employees at Cisco Finance about their organization's emotional culture, it became clear to management that fostering joy should be a priority. The survey didn't ask employees how they felt at work; it asked them what emotions they saw their coworkers expressing on a regular basis. (By having employees report on colleagues' emotions, researchers could obtain a more objective bird's-eye view of the culture.) It turned out that joy was one of the strongest drivers of employee satisfaction and commitment at the company—and more of it was needed to keep up engagement.

So management made joy an explicit cultural value, calling it "Pause for Fun." This signaled that it was an important outcome to track—just like productivity, creativity, and other elements of performance. Many companies use annual employee engagement surveys to gauge joy in the abstract, often in the form of job satisfaction and commitment to the organization. But Cisco Finance measured it much more specifically and is conducting follow-up surveys to track whether it is actually increasing. In addition, leaders throughout the organization support this cultural value with their own behavior—for example, by creating humorous videos that show them pausing for fun.

A Culture of Companionate Love

Another emotion we've examined extensively—one that's common in life but rarely mentioned by name in organizations—is *companionate love*. This is the degree of affection, caring, and compassion that employees feel and express toward one another.

In a 16-month study of a large long-term-care facility on the East Coast, we found that workers in units with strong cultures of companionate love had lower absenteeism, less burnout, and greater teamwork and job satisfaction than their colleagues in other units.[1] Employees also performed their work better, as demonstrated by more-satisfied patients, better patient moods, and fewer unnecessary trips to the emergency room. (Employees whose dispositions were positive to begin with received an extra performance boost from the culture.) The families of patients in units with stronger cultures of companionate love reported higher satisfaction with the facility. These results show a powerful connection between emotional culture and business performance.

Because this study took place in a health-care setting, we wondered whether companionate love matters only in "helping" industries. So we surveyed more than 3,200 employees in 17 organizations spanning seven industries: biopharmaceutical, engineering, financial services, higher education, public utilities, real estate, and travel. In organizations where employees felt and expressed companionate love toward one another, people reported greater job satisfaction, commitment, and personal accountability for work performance.

Creating an Emotional Culture

To cultivate a particular emotional culture, you'll need to get people to feel the emotions valued by the organization or team—or at least to behave as if they do. Here are three effective methods:

Harness What People Already Feel

Some employees will experience the desired emotions quite naturally. This can happen in isolated moments of compassion or gratitude, for example. When such feelings arise regularly, that's a sign you're building the culture you want. If people have them only periodically and need help sustaining them, you can try incorporating some gentle nudges during the workday. You might schedule some time for meditation, for instance; or provide mindfulness apps on people's work devices to remind them to simply breathe, relax, or laugh; or create a kudos board, like the one in an ICU we studied, where people can post kind words about other employees.

But what can you do about emotions that are toxic to the culture you're striving for? How can you discourage them when they already exist? Expecting people to "put a lid" on those feelings is both ineffective and destructive; the emotions will just come out later in counterproductive ways. It's important to listen when employees express their concerns so that they feel they are being heard. That's not to say you should encourage venting, or just let the emotions flow without attempting to solve the root problems. Indeed, research shows that extended venting can lead to poor outcomes. You're better off helping employees think about situations in a more constructive way. For example, loneliness, which can eat away at employee attitudes and performance, is best addressed through cognitive reappraisal—getting people to reexamine their views of others' actions. Considering plausible benign motivations for their colleagues' behavior will make them less likely to fixate on negative explanations that could send them into a spiral.

Model the Emotions You Want to Cultivate

A long line of research on emotional contagion shows that people in groups "catch" feelings from others through behavioral mimicry and subsequent changes in brain function.[2] If you regularly walk into a room smiling with high energy, you're much more likely to create a culture of joy than if you wear a neutral expression. Your employees will smile back and start to mean it.

But negative feelings, too, spread like wildfire. If you frequently express frustration, that emotion will infect your team members—and their team members, and so on—throughout the organization. Before you know it, you'll have created a culture of frustration.

So consciously model the emotions you want to cultivate in your company. Some organizations go a step further and explicitly ask employees to spread certain emotions. Ubiquity Retirement + Savings says, "Inspire happiness with contagious enthusiasm. Own your joy and lend it out." Vail Resorts says, "Enjoy your work and share the contagious spirit."

Get People to Fake It 'Til They Feel It

If employees don't experience the desired emotion at a particular moment, they can still help maintain their organization's emotional culture. That's because people express emotions both spontaneously and strategically at work. Social psychology research has long shown that individuals tend to conform to group norms of emotional expression, imitating others out of a desire to be liked and accepted. So employees in a strong emotional culture who would not otherwise feel and express the valued emotion will begin to demonstrate it—even if their initial motivation is to be compliant rather than to internalize the culture.

This benefits the organization, not just the individuals trying to thrive in it. In early anthropological studies of group rituals, strategic emotional expression was found to facilitate group cohesion by overpowering individual feelings and synchronizing interpersonal behavior.

So maintaining the appropriate culture sometimes entails disregarding what you are truly feeling. Through "surface acting," employees can display the valued emotion without even wanting to feel it. Surface acting isn't a long-term solution, though. Research shows that it can eventually lead to burnout—particularly in the absence of any outlet for authentic emotions.[3]

A better way to cultivate a desired emotion is through "deep acting." With this technique, people make a focused effort to feel a certain way—and then suddenly they do. Imagine that an employee at an accounting firm has a family emergency and requests a week off work at the height of tax audit season. Although his boss's first thought is *No—not now—no!* she could engage in deep acting to change her immediate feelings of justifiable panic into genuine caring and concern for her subordinate. By trying hard to empathize, saying "Of course, you should go be with your family!" and using the facial expressions, body language, and tone of voice she would use when actually feeling those emotions, she could coax herself into the real thing. She would also be modeling a desired behavior for the subordinate and the rest of the team.

Fortunately, all these ways of creating an emotional culture—whether they involve really feeling the emotion or simply acting that way—can reinforce one another and strengthen the culture's norms. People don't have to put on an act forever. Those who begin by expressing an emotion out of a desire to conform will start to actually feel it through emotional contagion. They'll also receive positive reinforcement for following the norms, which will make them more likely to demonstrate the emotion again.

Of course, the culture will be much stronger and more likely to endure if people truly believe in the values and assumptions behind it. Someone who is uncomfortable with an organization's emotional culture and has to keep pretending in order to be successful would probably be better off moving to a different work environment. Companies often have more than one emotional culture, so another unit or department might be a good fit. But if the culture is homogeneous, the employee may want to leave the company entirely.

Implementation Matters at All Levels

Just like other aspects of organizational culture, emotional culture should be supported at all levels of the organization. The role of top management is to drive it.

Leaders are often insufficiently aware of how much influence they have in creating an emotional culture. Traci Fenton is the founder and CEO of WorldBlu, a consulting firm that tackles fear at work. She shares this example: At one *Fortune* 500 company, unbeknownst to the CEO, senior employees regularly use text message codes to describe his nonverbal expressions of anger in meetings. "RED" means he is getting red in the face. "VEIN" means his veins are popping out. "ACP," which stands for "assume the crash position," means he is about to start throwing things. This leader is very effective at creating an emotional culture—but it's probably not the one he wants.

So don't underestimate the importance of day-to-day modeling. Large, symbolic emotional gestures are powerful, but only if they are in line with daily behavior. Senior executives can also shape an emotional culture through organizational practices. Take "compassionate firing," which is common at companies that build a strong culture of companionate love. Carlos Gutierrez, the vice president of R&D systems at Lattice Semiconductor, was deeply concerned about the impact of layoffs on his employees. He recognized that the traditional HR protocol of asking terminated employees to clean out their desks immediately and leave the premises would be especially painful to people who had worked side by side for 10–20 years. Along with his partners in HR and R&D, he implemented a protocol whereby employees had an extended time to say good-bye to their colleagues and to commemorate their time together at the company. Also, although two-thirds of the R&D workforce is outside the United States, Sherif Sweha, the corporate vice president of R&D, believed it was important for the affected team members in each region to receive the news from a senior leader face-to-face. So he and members of his staff flew to the company's sites in Asia to have in-person conversations with all the employees to be laid off—and also those who would remain with the company.

Though top management sets the first example and establishes the formal rules, middle managers and front-line supervisors ensure that the emotional values are consistently practiced by others. Because one of the biggest influences on employees is their immediate boss, the suggestions that apply to senior executives also apply to those managers: They should ensure that the emotions they express at work reflect the chosen culture, and they should speak explicitly about what is expected from employees.

It's also important to link the emotional culture to operations and processes, including performance management systems. At Vail Resorts, the culture of joy has been incorporated into the annual review, which indicates how well each employee integrates fun into the work environment and rates everyone on supporting behaviors, such as being inclusive, welcoming, approachable, and positive. Someone who exceeds expectations is described as not only taking part in the fun but also offering "recommendations to improve the work environment to integrate fun."

Decades' worth of research demonstrates the importance of organizational culture, yet most of it has focused on the cognitive component. As we've shown, organizations also have an emotional pulse, and managers must track it closely to motivate their teams and reach their goals.

Emotional culture is shaped by how all employees—from the highest echelons to the front lines—comport themselves day in and day out. But it's up to senior leaders to establish which emotions will help the organization thrive, model those emotions, and reward others for doing the same. Companies in which they do this have a lot to gain.

———————

Sigal Barsade is the Joseph Frank Bernstein Professor of Management at Wharton. **Olivia A. O'Neill** is an assistant professor of management at George Mason University and a senior scholar at the school's Center for the Advancement of Well-Being.

NOTES

1. Sigal Barsade and Olivia A. O'Neill, "What's Love Got to Do with It? A Longitudinal Study of the Culture of Companionate Love and Employee and Client Outcomes in a Long-Term Care Setting," *Administrative Science Quarterly* 59, no 4. (2014).

2. Sigal Barsade, "The Ripple Effect: Emotional Contagion and Its Influence on Group Behavior," *Administrative Science Quarterly* 47, no. 4 (2002).

3. Alicia A. Grandey, "When 'The Show Must Go On': Surface Acting and Deep Acting as Determinants of Emotional Exhaustion and Peer-Rated Service Delivery," *Academy of Management Journal* 46, no. 1 (February 2003): 86–96.

Index

Index

Index